ONCE UPON A RHYME

IMAGINATION FOR
A NEW GENERATION

Shropshire
Edited by Steve Twelvetree

CW00871675

10 July 2004

From
  Alaister

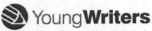 Young**Writers**
First published in Great Britain in 2004 by:
Young Writers
Remus House
Coltsfoot Drive
Peterborough
PE2 9JX
Telephone: 01733 890066
Website: www.youngwriters.co.uk

SB ISBN 1 84460 439 X

Foreword

Young Writers was established in 1991 and has been passionately devoted to the promotion of reading and writing in children and young adults ever since. The quest continues today. Young Writers remains as committed to engendering the fostering of burgeoning poetic and literary talent as ever.

This year's Young Writers competition has proven as vibrant and dynamic as ever and we are delighted to present a showcase of the best poetry from across the UK. Each poem has been carefully selected from a wealth of *Once Upon A Rhyme* entries before ultimately being published in this, our twelfth primary school poetry series.

Once again, we have been supremely impressed by the overall high quality of the entries we have received. The imagination, energy and creativity which has gone into each young writer's entry made choosing the best poems a challenging and often difficult but ultimately hugely rewarding task - the general high standard of the work submitted amply vindicating this opportunity to bring their poetry to a larger appreciative audience.

We sincerely hope you are pleased with our final selection and that you will enjoy *Once Upon A Rhyme Shropshire* for many years to come.

Contents

Holy Cross CE Junior School

Jack Taylor   36
Elspeth Cinnamond (11)   37
Jake Cook (8)   37
Becky Line (10)   38
Sian Owen (10)   39
Ewan Parry (9)   39
Chelsea Schaschke (10) & Connor Francis (11)   40
Tom Fewtrell (10)   40
Kate Teece (10)   41
Danie Price (11)   42
Ellen Kerr (8)   42
Tess Wauchope (11)   43
Eloise Sproul (7)   43
Eloise Davies (11)   44
Jake Mullinder   44
Luke Wilde (11)   45
Nathan Morgan   45
Ellie Gough (9)   46
Alex Collins (10)   46
Lisa Bennett (11)   47
Fiona Jaynes (7)   47
Ben Woolley-Henfield (11)   48
Ben Hadley (10)   49
Conor Crozier (11)   49
Demi Lewendon & Amy Owen (11)   50
Annabel Minton (9)   51
Lucy Cole (8)   52
George Hughes (7)   52

Longden CE Primary School

Evie Cartwright (9)   52
Callum Murtha (11)   53
Craig Davies (11)   53
James Pereira (11)   54
Gail Butler (10)   54
Kate Nixon (11)   55
Lucy Fotheringham (9)   55
Emma Greig (10)   56
Andrew Rotchell (10)   56
Rebecca Griffiths (10)   57

Lucy Lewis (9)	57
Emily Cox (10)	58
Alaister Watkins (10)	58
Josie Murtha (9)	59
Scott Dixon (11)	59
Oliver Emery (11)	60
Katy Jones (10)	60
Georgina Davies (10)	61
Cerian Abbott (10)	61
Lucy Hickson (10)	61
Sam W Rintoul (9)	62
Laura Price (9)	62
James Rowson (10)	63
Maddy Cartwright (11)	63
Laura Wallen (10)	64

Longlands Primary School

Abigail Louise Evans (8)	64
Jonathan Harrison (11)	65
Rebecca Jane Parton (11)	65
Millie Thomas (11)	66
Lauren Williams (8)	66
Courtney Duce (9)	67
Ainsley Almond (11)	67
Camilla Anne Edwards (10)	68
Dominic Sheridan (8)	68
Sarah Butter (11)	69
Elliott Bennett (10)	69
Paul K Clarke (9)	70
Jeffrey Pollard (8)	70
Bethany Cash (8)	71
Leigh Edwards (8)	71
Stacey Bradshaw (9)	72
Tyler Crump (8)	72
Andrew Blake (9)	73
Katie Dykes (9)	74
Chelsea Louise Barber (8)	75
Jasmine Humphrey (8)	76
Vanessa Blake (7)	77
Emma Henderson (7)	77
Kieron Evans (7)	77

Myddle CE Primary School

Taylor Page (9)	78
Marie Teleki (11)	78
Devan Morgan (10)	79
Emily Abrahams (9)	79
Zoe Croft (9)	80
Delphine Price (9)	80
Nathan Kavanagh (10)	81
Holly Steed (10)	81

Our Lady & St Oswald's Catholic Primary School

Laura Urbano (10)	82
Rachael Holbrook (7)	82
Lucy Hibbitt (10)	83
Sebastian Pierpoint (8)	83
Frances Carrasco (11)	84
Harriet Strefford (11)	84
Rebecca Jones (9)	85
Natalie Renwick (9)	85
Rebecca Ozanne (10)	86
Sarah Coxhead (10)	87
Amy Jones (9)	88
Isabelle Makin (8)	88
Zoë Davies (9)	89
Bethany Griffiths (8)	89
Ashley Davies (9)	90
Rosie Keaney (10)	90
Emily Bound (9)	91
Emma Harding (10)	91
Ebony Clay (9)	92
Rhianna Carrasco (9)	93
Hollie Jones (9)	94
Natalie Jones (9)	95
Nia Roberts (11)	96
Sophie Jennings (9)	96
Catherine Holbrook (9)	97
Tobie Clarke (8)	97

St John's RC Primary School, Bridgnorth

Jack Palmer (8)	98
Gary Ball (8)	98

Ben Meade (9)   114
Madeleine Robinson (8)   114
David Bowden (9)   114
Jasmine Oakley (9)   115
Molly Philpott (9)   115
Daniel Tait (7)   115
Georgina Hessey (9)   115
Bethany Foster (9)   116
Sam Kieran Day (8)   116
Kimberley Rose Gillett (7)   116
Chloe Warde (7)   116
Caroline Knight & Will Thompson (9)   117

Sir Alexander Fleming Primary School
Megan Bright (7)   117
Tara Ellis-Jeffries (10)   118
Sharna Cottey (8)   118
Alex Hitch (10)   119
Tilly May Perry (9)   119
Kelly Abbott (10)   120
Liam Melhuish (8)   120
Kane Regan (10)   121
Sean Davies (11)   121
Ben Perry (11)   122
Shaun Coldicutt (11)   122
Jamie Bright (11)   123
Laura Churm (9)   123
Casey Wells (10)   124
Jessica-Paris Stokes (9)   124
Bethany Luter (10)   125
Nicole Doyle (11)   125
Lisa Simpkins (11)   126
Andrew Stewart (11)   127
Jordan Needle (11)   128
Kimberley Roberts (10)   128
Layla Hughes (11)   129
Daniel Gill (11)   129
Jaimelea Morgan (10)   130
Katie Jane Webb (8)   130
Sarah Westwood (11)   131
Emma Baker (8)   131

The Poems

An Odd Kettle Of Fish

The teacher said the boy
'was as daft as a brush'.
(He was very good at sweeping up).

My mum said,
'Hold your tongue.'
(It felt horrible)

Some people bottle up
their feelings.
(Mine wouldn't stay in)

My friend drives me to distraction.
(I catch the train back)

I put my foot in it.
(I couldn't get it out)

My mum said I am a pain in the neck.
(I gave her some painkillers).

Lauren Walker (10)
Albrighton County Junior School

The Great Sharks

Camouflaged at the bottom like a Thompson gun ready to fire.
Swimmers lie in the sea. 'The shark!'
Eating dead fish like a mean highwayman.
Rushing through the sea like a speedboat.
The shark is a machine, breathing and killing.
The shark swims, swims, swims,
The shark swims into the deep, dark blue sea!
His soft, silky, swishy tail rules the Pacific Ocean.

Thomas Talbot (10)
Albrighton County Junior School

The White Tiger

There you are
ready to pounce,
watching through the long grass
stretching your legs
and curling your toes
twitching your whiskers
and licking your lips.
There he watches
very silently
then suddenly you *jump!*
right out from behind a tree
like an erupting volcano
and scratches the little mouse
because you're a sly white tiger.
Long hairy legs and big puffy paws
deep blue eyes
and massive white teeth
some little silver whiskers
and very furry skin.

Jamie Byrne (10)
Albrighton County Junior School

The Scorpion

There you sit,
On the sand.
You're a landmine
With your lethal sting.
You move so swiftly,
Almost silent,
Yet deadly.

Gareth Cobham (9)
Albrighton County Junior School

Lullaby

Lay down your sweet head,
let your tired eyes
carefully close on the day.

Lay down your sweet head,
let your sleepy head sink softly down
into the depths of your pillow.

Close your eyes,
let your little legs sink to the end of the bed
and back into your dream.

Lay down your sweet head,
let your tired mind drift softly
into nothing and nowhere.

Lay down your sweet head,
let your arms rest
till the summer day is done.

Catriona Neumann (8)
Albrighton County Junior School

The Lion

As the lion waits for its prey at the end of the day
he creeps carefully through the golden grass,
his furry coat as hot as the sun,
he strikes like lightning,
the carnivore grabs his prey by the neck,
the zebra's head is a wreck,
the lion roars and carries his dead prey back to his den,
his chin like the bristles on the bottom of a soggy, spiky brush.
As he pauses under a shady tree next to the dead body
he rests with a bloody face.

Jonathan Maddock (10)
Albrighton County Junior School

You!

You!
Your cheeks are like
great lumpy tomatoes.
You!
Your fingers are like
great big bananas.
You!
Your fingernails are like
smooth, sharp glass.
You!
Your knuckles are like
high pointed hills.
You!
Your knees are like
huge, large caps.
You!
Your fists are like
the hard force of the wind.
You!
Your elbows are like
pointed bowls.
You!
Your teeth are like
moulded sweets.

Kelsey Brodie (7)
Albrighton County Junior School

The Flying Fish

There you are gliding across the water like a boat.
Whoosh! Like a jet in the air with a crash when you land
And you zoom by other fish in the Atlantic Ocean
As they follow you through the weeds.

Kallum Giles (9)
Albrighton County Junior School

The Dolphin

The dolphin's slippery, smooth, soft skin.
Gliding in the air.
Speeding as fast as lightning strikes!
Above the huge, blue, cold waves.
Swimming under the great fishes,
Under the boats they go.
Speaking as loud as a choir singing.
Flapping their big grey-bluey fins.
Waves like twisted ribbon,
Like a giant kite in the windy air.
Swimming like waves in the sea,
Going anywhere you want to go
In the giant blue sea, in freedom.

Katherine Kyriacou (9)
Albrighton County Junior School

Sleep Little One

Sleep little one,
Let your tired eyes
Rest on the day.
Sleep little one,
Let your sweet head
Sink, slow down
Into the depths of your pillow.
Sleep little one,
Let your golden mind
Drift away into nothing and nowhere.
Sleep little one,
Let your lovely tongue be still,
Till the spring day blossoms.

Jessica Roberts (8)
Albrighton County Junior School

You!

You!
Your cheeks are like great lumpy pillowcases.
You!
Your fingers are like tiny fat bananas.
You!
Your fingernails are like rough, sharp glass.
You!
Your knuckles are like long, blunt hills.
You!
Your knees are like red flaming fire.
You!
Your fists are like the weak, soft force of the wind.
You!
Your elbows are like loud big hammer blows.
You!
Your teeth are like green, big apples.

Tyler Carrington (7)
Albrighton County Junior School

Think About It

As red as a shiny postbox
As slow as a tiny tortoise
As flat as a flowing stream
As bright as a birthday boy
As busy as a guard dog
As fit as a gymnastic Mr Goodridge
As good as a little girl
As quiet as class one working
As loud as a Chinese gong drum
As fast as a greyhound.

Jason Beattie (8)
Albrighton County Junior School

Light

I feel scared and trapped in the dark.
I feel really dull deep down.
I feel I can't breathe, inside my heart beats.
I feel I can't move because I'm so frightened.
I feel spooked out.
I feel happy, excited because it's sunset.
I'm glad and cheerful.
I'm really pleased and delighted.
I feel all merry and jolly.
I feel ungrateful.
I feel moody.
I feel unhappy.
I hear fireworks.
I hear loud noises.
I feel dozy, cross and evil.
I feel scared of great big stories.
I feel all light and sunny.
I feel all shiny, colourful.

Laura Harris (8)
Albrighton County Junior School

The Snake

There you hang,
Down from the tree.
A metal chain,
In your jungle camouflage.
As fast as a stone from a catapult,
Like a pellet from a gun.

Callum Ibbs-George (9)
Albrighton County Junior School

You!

You!
Your cheeks are like great, lumpy, cherry tomatoes.
You!
Your fingers are like giant, dirty bananas.
You!
Your fingernails are like jagged, scary rocks.
You!
Your knuckles are like giant crooked hills.
You!
Your kneecaps are like huge alarm clocks.
You!
Your fist is like rough lightning.
You!
Your elbows are like the blades on a steel sword.
You!
Your teeth are like black coal.

James Sturgess (8)
Albrighton County Junior School

The Giraffe

Your neck as high as a crane,
So you can reach up to the tall branches
And chomp, chomp, chomp
On the crunchy leaves of the tree.
You live in the hot horizon
Staring at the light of the world, the sun.
You're the great, gorgeous giraffe,
You are as quiet as can be,
You will always be the glorious giraffe,
You dance to the classical music
While you're munching on the tree
And your head swings to and fro.

Brittany Gillham (9)
Albrighton County Junior School

Lullaby

Gently
let your tired eyes
rest on the day

Sleep quietly
let your little head
sink, drift down
into the depths of your pillow

Close your eyes
let your tiny legs
crawl to the end of the bed
and back into your dream

Peacefully
let your brave mind
drift slowly into nothing
and nowhere

My body, rest
let your small body be still
till the bright day blossoms.

Liam Hansen (8)
Albrighton County Junior School

The Cheetah

Fast and sly, her fur has spots
like big black dots in a sieve,
it chases like a snake after its prey,
it's as fast as a F1 car going 100 miles per hour,
when the horizon rises the cheetah is hunting
for prey for her cubs.

Edward Aldridge (10)
Albrighton County Junior School

Megan

My aunty Ruth, this is the truth,
She is a lovely lady.
At Christmas time quite by surprise
She had a little baby.

Her name was Megan
She is a love,
She is as soft as a little dove.

In the day she sleeps away,
When fed and changed she's put to lay,
But when night-time comes
She cries and cries
And gives her mummy baggy eyes.

She came six weeks early
With hair so dark and curly,
But the doctor says she's doing fine
And my aunty and my cousin are mine, all mine.

Ashleigh Medlyn (8)
Albrighton County Junior School

The Elephant

There he gracefully heaves . . .
Stomp, stomp, stomp
His crinkled, blotchy, brown, muddy skin
Like the minced beef rushing out of a fresh warm cottage pie
His long sharp tusks and his yellow dirty teeth
Both like old knives rotting in a worn out garage . . .
And in the far, far distance, when the horizon is high
You can see this crinkled, coated creature heading northwards.

Jessica Flavell (10)
Albrighton County Junior School

You!

You!
Your cheeks are like great, grand pillowcases.
You!
Your fingers are like tiny fat bananas.
You!
Your fingernails are like sparkly, soft grass.
You!
Your knuckles are like long, blunt hills.
You!
Your knees are like red flaming fire.
You!
Your fists are like the weak force of the wind.
You!
Your elbows are like steady and calm hammer blows.
You!
Your teeth are like sweaty sweetcorn.

Sophie Sankey (7)
Albrighton County Junior School

Light

Rainbow, happy
Moon, joyful
Fire, danger
Traffic lights, scared
Candle, quiet
Lightning, frightening
River, calm
Firework, amazed
Flowers, peaceful
Shadows, spooky
Lighthouse, spooky
Devil, evil.

Charlotte Davies (8)
Albrighton County Junior School

The Lion Cub

He sits there silently,
tired, weak and starving,
eating like an empty jam jar.
Moving in the blinding sun,
his fur like a worn out doormat,
his eyes like hollow grapes,
he's taken every last bit of energy,
but he's still stuck in the Sahara Desert.

Hayley Carrington (9)
Albrighton County Junior School

As . . .

As red as a spitting fire
As slow as a tiny tortoise
As flat as a piece of paper
As bright as a blazing sun
As busy as a bustling bus
As fit as an Olympic runner
As good as friendship
As quiet as slippery snow.

Ross MacDonald (7)
Albrighton County Junior School

The Male Fox

Foxes are intelligent animals
They are as fast as a Ferrari
Their fur is as smooth as a blanket
Their teeth are as sharp and dirty as a crab's claw,
Their whiskers are as fuzzy as a fuzzy piece of string,
Its long, dirty red fur is as red as the sun.

Joshua Bell (10)
Albrighton County Junior School

The Rainbow Fish

There you swim through the warm clear water
Striped like a deckchair
Outside in the sun your colours change
And you show how multicoloured you really are
You glide through the water
Glistening and glowing
Proud of your own appearance.

Josie Causer (9)
Albrighton County Junior School

My Pony

My pony . . .
Jumps and plays and rolls
In the long green grass
And canters and gallops
As free as the wind
As fast as a speedboat.

Toni Whitehouse (9)
Albrighton County Junior School

The Koala Bear

There you sit all day, every day,
Just hanging there eating eucalyptus leaves,
Looking onto the horizon,
Watching the blazing sun.
As smooth as silk
And fur as soft as cotton wool.

Lauren Withers (10)
Albrighton County Junior School

As . . .

As red as a pot of boiling lava
As slow as a time clock
As flat as a window
As bright as a blazing hot sun
As busy as a time machine
As fit as a champion boxer
As good as the human world
As quiet as an ant.

Connor Gillham (7)
Albrighton County Junior School

As Red As A Pencil Case

As red as a pencil case
As slow as falling white snow
As flat as a carpet
As bright as car lights
As busy as a printer
As fit as a dog
As good as golden gold
As quiet as a marksman.

Joshua Gladman (8)
Albrighton County Junior School

The Dolphin

Swishes and splashes in the deep blue sea,
Suddenly shooting up through the air,
Like an arrow released from a bow.

Emma-Jane Cottle (9)
Albrighton County Junior School

The Snake

There you are dangling off the tree,
You look as strong as a chain.
Your skin is as yellow as a banana
And your hiss is like a broken tap.
Mean!

Rachel Johnson (10)
Albrighton County Junior School

Winter Has Decorated The Garden

Lady Winter has decorated the garden
The snow has sprinkled down a life of winter,
The snow was a layer of icing sugar
Lying on the grass.

The trees look like a crown of ice,
Glittering with gems,
Lady Winter is here. She walks around the garden path,
She glides swiftly throughout the winter's day
And carries it down the garden,
She was walking through a white winter wonderland
When winter has decorated the garden.

Robins are huddled on a lonely branch
She has made the grass sit up, in frost, in curls,
She looks at the pond turned to ice,
It reflected her image like looking at a polished mirror.

Lady Winter would walk
Along the grass,
Wherever her feet would move
You hear a crunch of ice
Being cracked,
When winter has decorated the garden.

Rebeca-Emelia Loureda (10)
Captain Webb Primary School

Me And You

Sitting on the pavement, rain lashing at my face,
Sheltered by an old battered box.
My eyes are fixed on the perfect home,
The home of a girl with a family.

Like a freezing snowman, totally alone,
Clutched in a trap of bitter weather.
I am wishing I was sitting by a roaring fire,
Enjoying and reading a book.
Ripping, tearing and shredding off wrapping paper,
From a box crammed full of presents:
Instead I have a box full of rubbish,
Hoping to find some sort of warmth within.

A huge table filled with a feast,
Ready to eat.
While I hope to find a scrap of food,
To help me survive just one more day.

Victoria Green (11)
Captain Webb Primary School

The Night I Saw Winter

Winter swiftly danced upon the frosted grass,
Covering it with ice,
She sprinkled snow like icing, across the willow trees,
Freezing and frosting as she goes,
She drew one mighty breath and blasted it all out,
Causing the air to freeze and shimmer,
The air around her blew wildly,
As she leaped and jumped with excitement,
'Winter is free, winter is free!'
The words carried across the breeze
As her image faded away into nothing.

James Budd (11)
Captain Webb Primary School

Warm And Cold

It's freezing cold,
Icicles hang from the windows,
As sharp as knives.

It's snowing,
It looks like a white blanket,
Like millions of cotton wool balls.

People cosy in their beds,
Like mice in their beds,
Sleeping tight.

Animals resting in their warm beds,
Thinking about their day,
Ignoring any noise.

Vicky Tranter (11)
Captain Webb Primary School

Hot And Cold

Cold makes me feel sad and cold,
On those frosty winter nights.
As I lie in my frozen thin sheets,
While the chilly wind blows
Through the cracks in the windows.

Hot makes me feel cosy and happy,
On those warm summer nights.
While I snuggle up to thick sheets,
As the central heating beams
Its warmth through the pipes.

Chloe May (11)
Captain Webb Primary School

Winter Has Decorated The Garden

Lady Winter's here,
Her blue-white colour of cold is deadly to the touch.
She has printed patterns on the delicate snowflake.
As she swiftly glides past the bush, her fingertips turn it to ice.
The water fountain is having a nap frozen for winter.
The grass is ready for bed,
Tucked up under its thick, white blanket of snow.
The holly bush is bleeding red.
The pond ice-bound,
As the cold-hearted Lady Winter
Whispers icicles which hang from gutters.
Hedgehogs furling, for winter's here.

Ami Richards (10)
Captain Webb Primary School

Cold Finger

The windows glow bright amber,
the chimney smokes a cigar
and all is still.

A dark shadow limps down the street,
with something dripping off its coat,
gripping something in its claw,

screaming,

crying

and all shivers.

Billy Fletcher (11)
Captain Webb Primary School

Love (Kenning)

Sweet kisser
Moonlight dancer
Heart breaker
Time waster
Eye flutterer
Rose bringer
Head acher
Sadness awakener
Nightclub parties
Groovy smoothies
Tear trickler
Heart blister
Lovely picnics
Love creator.

Laura Edwards (10)
Captain Webb Primary School

Winter Has Decorated The Garden

Winter has decorated the garden.
The pond is frozen with ice,
Reflecting her image like a polished mirror,
Her pale skin is as soft as snow,
Her glittering eyes are hailstones,
Silver teardrops tickle down her icy cheeks,
Snowflakes float from her parted lips,
Her cold breath drifts through the silent air,
Her pointed icicle fingers cut through the sky,
Freezing all they touch.

Charlotte Carline (11)
Captain Webb Primary School

Love

Love is a bond,
Anyone can have love.
If you leave your children
Without telling where you are going,
Your love will be gone.
Love has one main thing,
In love is trust.
You can't see love,
You can't smell love
But you can feel it.
Love is a kiss on a cheek.
Love is a hug.
Love is a shoulder to cry on.

Chad Stevenson (10)
Hadnall CE Primary School

Dolphin

It leaps up out of the water's depths,
Suspended in the air,
Its subtle landing takes it back down to the sea.

The sun beams onto the gleaming ocean's surface,
Making a sunny spell,
It tries to show off its sleek, grey skin,
By communicating and trying to tell.

Its eerie sound that's sent round the sea
Gathers its family together,
If it is scared or lost
It will always find its mother.

But only if people allow it to live its life
Free!

Gemma Higgins (11)
Hadnall CE Primary School

A Pike's Life

One Saturday afternoon,
Fat Pike was hiding in the weed beds
trying to avoid being caught.
She kept as still as she could
and didn't come to the surface,
waiting for smaller fish to pass by
to eat. Fat Pike followed a 10lb pike
who was chasing little roach and perch . . .
As quick as a cheetah
she bit the 10lb pike's tail by mistake,
she was hungry,
then she saw a small, juicy pike
sleeping in the sunlight.
Fat Pike swam slowly and quietly
towards her lunch . . .
Full and tired Fat Pike went back
to her comfortable, dark weed bed.
It's a pike's life!

Richard Bowers (10)
Hadnall CE Primary School

My Thoughts About War

I feel war is silly
But it can be very serious.
I know people do it for their country
But sometimes they just do it for fame.
I see it on the TV and it doesn't look that bad
But in reality it is much worse.
It makes me feel angry
When people die for no reason.
So, please stop war
So everybody can live a happy life.

Tom Smith (10)
Hadnall CE Primary School

Pollution

Animals dying every day,
Diseases spreading everywhere.
People using the world like a bin.
The swishing sea.
The green grass.
The fresh soil
Will disappear
In a pile of crisp packets
And garbage.
There will be no fun,
Nowhere to play,
The world will be dull.
So let's stop pollution
Before it's too late.

Adam Wilson (10)
Hadnall CE Primary School

Romans

The Romans
Took over most of Europe
I felt glad
The Romans aren't around today!
Defeating the Celts
It was easy
In battle, the Celts were half naked
Men and women watched gladiators fight
They watched them fight fierce animals
Roman towns can still be found today
But now they are just remains
Caesar was stabbed by his friends
And the Roman Empire fell.

Daniel Hughes (9)
Hadnall CE Primary School

Night And Day

Night
The moon, as white as a torch.
The night, as dark as coal.
The bats fly as the hedgehogs
Awaken from their deep sleep.
The foxes come out to find food
For their young cubs.

Day
The sun, as bright as can be.
The light is a dazzling flame.
The birds come out to sing
As the rabbits hop around in the fields.
The creatures and insects come out
To feed on the plants.

The end of the day
Is the start of the next night.

Aoife Marsh (10)
Hadnall CE Primary School

A Lazy Shark's Life

Once I met a lazy shark in an aquarium.
He would sleep all day.
Never to come out to play in the rocks.
Never to come out to eat.
Although he may look like a fearsome lion
Ready to kill buffalo
He is actually soft as a mouse on the inside.
So he's just sleeping all day.
Never to come out.

Thomas Watkin (9)
Hadnall CE Primary School

Animals

My neck is tall
like my four legs
I'm yellow like the sun
bat-brown like mud
I eat from the best leaves
from the tallest trees.

In Africa
we run around
in the hot weather
and on the soft sand.
Guess who I am?

My nose is long
my ears are big
I'm grey as slate
but I'm as wrinkly as the leaves I eat
when I put my foot down
I sound like a drum
so when we all move
it sounds like an orchestra.

In Africa
we run around
in the hot weather
and on soft sand.
Guess who I am?

My head is surrounded by fur
I have sharp claws on my padded feet
I'm as yellow as the sun
but as fast as can be
I'm the king of the country, that's me.

In Africa
we run around
in the hot weather
and on soft sand.
Guess who I am?

Bethan Lloyd (10)
Hadnall CE Primary School

Family Poem

Family are lovely.
My family gives my heart a warm glow.
I feel happy and wanted
In my home with my family.
It's warm and cosy.
It wouldn't be right
Without arguments and being told off.
I feel upset when I get told off,
But I know it's because I have done wrong.
When my family have arguments
It's like a volcano erupting.
They start as nothing much but grow and grow.
When my family are happy it's fantastic
And that makes me feel wonderful.

Jessica Deer (11)
Hadnall CE Primary School

The Cheetah

His speed like a bolt of lightning
Furiously scampering across the sandy plain
His mind focusing on his prey
As he stalks slyly through the long, scorched grass
A powerful leap sends him flying
As he pounces on his squealing prey
A sudden cry comes from the creature
It tries to escape!
But then a wave of silence fills the air
The cheetah has succeeded.

Abigail Bebb (9)
Hadnall CE Primary School

Listen

'In my day, children were seen but not heard'.
'You know, I don't like children
Who decide what they're allowed to do'.
'What part of be quiet don't you understand'.
It's all . . .
Listen, listen, listen, listen.
Now you listen!
Why should I listen to you?
You have no real power!
Why should I listen to you?
You don't and won't listen to me!
You act like you're God
You act like only you matter
As if you don't realise!
As if you don't realise
Just how self-obsessed you are!
As if you don't realise
Just how irritating you are!
It's all . . .
Listen, listen, listen, listen!

Ceara Marsh (10)
Hadnall CE Primary School

Snow

When I tread through the snow
It makes me feel cold.
It makes me feel like I am going to freeze.
When I throw snowballs at the windows
My mum says, 'Stop it!'
When I skate on the ice I always fall over.
When I touch the snow it is really soft.
The snow is just like a pure white sheet.
When I grab a lot of snow it feels really heavy.

Laura Hotchkiss (10)
Hadnall CE Primary School

Life

Everyone has a life!
Life is great, you have your own mind.
You think what you want,
Do what you want
And you still don't have to share it,
You have your own things.
Like what you like,
You can do what you want
And be who you are.

Madeleine Rowlinson (9)
Hadnall CE Primary School

My Skatewear Top

My skatewear top is lovely,
It fits me like a glove,
It feels so nice on me,
It's cool says my bruv.

It gives me this nice feeling,
A feeling to go and play,
I really like this feeling,
I could wear it any day.

My mum thinks it's a nice top
And so does my dad,
My brother really wants one,
It makes me feel quite mad.

I really like my skater top
And I'm really glad it's mine!

James Trow (10)
Hinstock Primary School

A Poem To Be Spoken Quietly

It was so silent,
That I heard the autumn leaves,
Being torn from the trees,
Like a pair of gloves.

It was so silent,
That the snail's shell,
Was ripped off,
Like a hat.

It was so silent,
That the tide left the beach,
As smoothly,
As taking socks off.

It was so silent,
That I heard the old shell,
Of a crab,
Breaking like an old shoe.

It was so silent,
That I could hear the darkness,
Leaving the morning sky,
Like an anorak gradually being unzipped.

Fern Little (9)
Hinstock Primary School

I Love Snow

I love snow
Even though it's really cold.
It doesn't mould
It blows in the cold.
It melts on the window
The sun comes out
It melts.

Aaron Pritchard (9)
Hinstock Primary School

Daisy The Dog

Daisy is a funny little fellow
She is black, white and yellow.

She lives around the corner
With my friend Lorna.

Daisy has some rather naughty habits
Like chasing my pet rabbits.

Bill and Ben had a rather nasty fright
Last Friday night.

After her naughty adventure she was glad to get by the Aga
And pinch a bit of my dad's lager.

Most of the time Daisy is good
And enjoys going for walks with me and my dog, Pud.

Today is Saturday, hip hip hooray!
No school today!

Lorna and I are off to the park
With Pud, Daisy and our friend Mark
What a lark.

Elizabeth Jackson (8)
Hinstock Primary School

Christmas Tree

I like the way Christmas tree glitters
by the sparkling tinsel
and I see the bouncing baubles
and a lovely star on top.
There's a brown pot at the bottom.
When the tree goes out if feels lonely
and you feel like the room is empty.

Daniel Pickstone (10)
Hinstock Primary School

My Senses

I can hear,
It is really near,
I can see,
There's a bee,
I can smell,
It's a shell,
Help! It's a bear,
Take care,
They are quite rare,
I can feel,
It's real,
I can taste,
It's some paste,
So say *Yippee!*
We can hear, smell, taste,
See and feel.

Anna Bowen (8)
Hinstock Primary School

My Cat Mog

My cat is called Mog,
She spits and hisses at the neighbour's dog.
Mog has shiny, soft fur,
When I give her a brush she starts to purr.

Mog is a tabby cat,
She loves to play with her toy bat.
She runs into the kitchen and jumps up her scratch post,
She loves the smell of the Sunday roast.

Sometimes she brings in a mouse or two,
Once she caught a long-nosed shrew.

Emily Furber (10)
Hinstock Primary School

Animals

Animals are all over the world,
The ones in the sea are mostly curled.
When you go out and look up high,
You'll see a bird in the sky.

Limpets all just stick to the ground,
But there are some that have never been found.
Hissing snakes give you a scare,
But it's even worse with spiders there.

Some are slimy like a grub,
I'd hate to see them in the pub.
When driving down the street at night,
You'd probably see a fox in the light.

So when you see an animal at night,
Be careful because it might *bite!*

Ben Jordan (11)
Hinstock Primary School

Gleaming Snow

I love the snow,
I like to watch it blow.

It gleams so bright,
Especially at night.

It flows in the air,
But does not tear.

The snowflakes fall down,
Into the watchful town.

The snow is great,
And so elegant that I just can't wait.

Emily Lyons (9)
Hinstock Primary School

The Unicorn Dance

The unicorn dance, the unicorn dance,
Where the unicorns jump and twirl and prance,
The unicorns love to go to the dance,
They never usually get the chance,
To dance, to dance.

The unicorn dance, the unicorn dance,
You will never get to take a glance,
It is a secret where they dance,
Where they prance and twirl and take the chance,
To dance, to dance.

Holly Fletcher (10)
Hinstock Primary School

My Game Boy Advance SP

I love my Game Boy Advance SP,
It's always really fun,
I'm on it all the time,
Even when there's lots of sun.

I love my Game Boy Advance SP,
I'll always love that thing,
My favourite game is Pokémon,
But my best one's lost its wing.

Michael Pickstone (9)
Hinstock Primary School

The Giant

A giant can be very nasty,
They have very big mouths to eat
Little children who may enter
The castle which is up the street.

Alex Whittingham (8)
Hinstock Primary School

A To H

A is for ants,
Ants in my pants.

B is for bats,
Who spy on cats.

C is for creatures,
Who come out in the dark.

D is for dog,
That has a loud bark.

E is for elephants,
So big and strong.

F is for fish,
And they can't go wrong.

G is for giraffe,
So big and tall.

H is for horse,
Who likes to jump a wall.

Stephanie Walley (10)
Hinstock Primary School

Naughty Jack

Jack climbs through fences,
And is such a greedy thing,
He doesn't like hay,
His birthday's in May.

Lucy Gilliland-Simon (10)
Hinstock Primary School

My Mum

My mum was beautiful and sweet,
My mum always kept things neat.
My mum was as elegant as a swan,
My mum always knew what was going on.
My mum had grey-blue eyes like mine,
My dad says that they would always shine.
My mum threw parties all the time,
My mum has shown me what's mine.
Until I was 3,
She was there for me.
Then the crash,
It was such a dash.
I left with a scar,
She lost her life.

Alice Ratheram (11)
Hinstock Primary School

My Grandad, Norman

My grandad, Norman
He always loses his teeth.
When he does he yells
Just like a thief.

When he wakes up in the morning
He says it's the dawning.
Then he watches telly
Before he puts on his welly.

J J Lutner (9)
Hinstock Primary School

Seasons

Winter is really fun,
Even without that bright, bright sun,
The best thing is snowball fights,
But the weather is not good for kites,
Snow falls down,
On the ground,
All around.

Spring is the new year,
And winter is on our rear,
Pretty flowers start to grow,
Because from past experience they all know,
Summer is the next season,
And for that reason,
Their buds start to grow,
As the river water begins to flow.

Summer is really hot,
But boring it is not,
Relaxing on those lovely beaches,
Looking at all summer's exquisite features,
Trees' branches reaching way up high,
Trying to reach the very sky.

Now it's autumn and the wind is blowing,
And the river water will soon stop flowing,
Soon enough animals will run,
When their storage is all done,
They hide their food in a safe place,
While they make a cosy base.

Gregory Pereira Sgrol (11)
Hinstock Primary School

Rosie

My cat is called Rosie.
When you hold her
You can hear her purr.
She is black
You can see her playing
With her little toys.
She likes waiting for her food
And she plays with you
And her toys.
But when boys touch her
She hides away
In her bed.
She has blue eyes
And her little paws are sweet.

Georgina Abbotts (10)
Hinstock Primary School

A Snowy Winter

The ice shines on the floor,
With people shivering in the cold.

Icicles dangling from a freezing deserted cave,
The sand squelching wet and cold on the beach.

The snow on the floor like a large white rug,
Made a snowman with a carrot for his nose.

I'm in bed as snug as can be,
People all looking extremely cheerful.

Snow on the gatepost is a big white handkerchief
A big white handkerchief.

Jack Taylor
Holy Cross CE Junior School

Element Poem

The Wind is lonely and sorrowful
She sits alone every day
She weeps and howls all day long
Longing for a friend.

The Sea is a show-off
Doing his gymnastics
As the Sand applauds with glee.

The Moon is a playful girl
She's always playing hide-and-seek
Amongst the clouds
With the stars.

Fire is a bully
Who destroys everything in his way
He'll hurt you if you touch him
So everyone keeps out of his way.

Elspeth Cinnamond (11)
Holy Cross CE Junior School

Nell

My dog is called Nell,
She is really swell,
She is difficult to see at night,
Because she is more black than white,
When she is in the hall,
She likes to play with her ball,
She has got four feet,
And she's really sweet,
Golly! She is a Border collie.

Jake Cook (8)
Holy Cross CE Junior School

My School Poem

The lonely, sleepy bag loiters, boredom in his eyes,
Pining for his owner to hasten back once more,
And bring back some happiness into his little heart.
The dainty window sits alone,
While singing people stare,
Hoping that no one will come and break her fragile bones.
The haughty pictures perch with pride,
Anticipating the arrival of their next audience,
Preparing to be praised once more.

The neat, tidy CD player slouches, looking for his next victim to
terrorise.
The books stand in lines wondering who's going to be picked next for
the big job.
The colourful radiator sits alone longing for someone to turn him on
and keep him warm.

The blue trampoline waits for people to come and play with him.
The lazy fire extinguisher drinks and drinks all day till he has to blow.
The plates scream as children bash and bang the plates with knives
and forks.
The brown and white trays wait before kids come and fight over them.
The blinds hang all day watching the kids play and play.

The displays never want to be put away so they always look their best.
The dusty lost property boxes sit alone all day
getting fuller and fuller till they overflow
The gleaming lights stand out from the rest until
people kick balls at their pretty faces.

Becky Line (10)
Holy Cross CE Junior School

The Moon

He stands behind the cushion blankets,
Waiting for someone to come and hold him,
He longs and longs to have someone to love,
He changes and changes every night.

He comes out when it's dark and gloomy,
Looking for someone to watch over him,
He glides in and out of the cotton buds,
Hanging around the deep, blue sky.

Floating around like he hasn't got a life,
Feeling more helpless as the night goes on,
He melts apart more and more every night,
Wishing and wishing for some love.

Sian Owen (10)
Holy Cross CE Junior School

A Different World

I look out of the window,
The world is changed.
What has happened to the pond?
Who has dropped this piece of glass on it?
Who is throwing this white confetti?
Who is the culprit for this disaster?

Is somebody angry with me?
Have I been banished to a different land?
The trees are as bare as an old cellar.
I feel so scared,
My legs have turned to jelly.

Ewan Parry (9)
Holy Cross CE Junior School

A School Journey

The door of the classroom yawns as she opens wider.
Suddenly she speaks as someone knocks her on her back.
At half-past three she yawns again.
She goes to sleep until it is time for her to wake.
Ready for another day.

The friendly cloakroom shakes with joy
As woolly coats fling themselves on to outstretched metal hands.
Smiling doors wave to and fro while thousands of feet rush past.

The hall feels empty, tired and lonely,
After its face has been bashed and bruised
By thundering feet.
His strong and colourful friend, the climbing frame, stands guard.
Gentle hands brush over gleaming white keys.
Sound fills his mind and he feels relaxed and happy.

The knives and forks stand to attention as the trays clash about.
The spoons stand there shaking, ready to be dunked into puddings.
Suddenly hands grab trays and water eats them up ready
for another victim.

The patient trolley stands waiting and a boy comes and pushes it.
The trolley says, 'Hooray, I am the king.'
The TV with his blank face stares into space, waiting for
someone to push his buttons.

Chelsea Schaschke (10) & Connor Francis (11)
Holy Cross CE Junior School

The Door

The chatterbox door
has his conversations with
other items in
the corridor, while people
walk in his territory.

Tom Fewtrell (10)
Holy Cross CE Junior School

My Poem

The super, silver CD player waited patiently, contemplating his next
move when suddenly he jumped with joy
As a girl fed him a shiny treat
His eyes twinkled, his head spun round
As his buttons were pressed and his cheeks filled with sound.

The lonely, left-out computer looks up all the facts
But he gets bored with sitting there all day
And he wishes to go out and play
But what can he do to change the way he is.

The beautiful, big-headed banner knows that everyone admires her
She boasts every hour, every day
But she walks alone with pride and glory
And she thinks she's the most elegant of them all.

The courageous, heroic trampoline
Is always up for adventure
But when it's night he creeps out and talks to his mate, the apparatus.

The naughty, lively cutlery slink out at night, they get out the food and
wait in excitement for it to cook.
Then when it's cooked they shout, 'Hooray!' and crawl back to their
place, ready for another day.

The impatient, bored fire extinguisher lingers for something to happen
He scratches his head and talks to himself, but still nothing seems
to emerge
He hears the fire bell and shouts with ecstasy, but still he is not used.

The blissful, peace-loving blinds never want to fight
They stand and stare at passers-by
As they quarrel and argue
And mutters, 'They'll never learn.'

Kate Teece (10)
Holy Cross CE Junior School

The School Comes To Life

The whiteboard stands on the wall all through the day,
And longs for the children to go out and play.
It tickles her when they write on her face,
She loves to be in this cosy place.

The computer's mouse scurries around and looks for a bed,
So he can rest for the busy day ahead.
He finds a mat to spread on and softly goes to sleep
Until the computer turns on for all the kids next week!

When she hears the frightful bell she gives some little sighs,
As the children stamp upon her face she stands down low and cries.

She has to wait for a single spill,
Or a cup of coffee from the staffroom's sill.

They are very muscly men,
And each are only ten.
Their job is to hold the beam
Which isn't as heavy as you seem.

The banner stares at the children while he's up so high,
The children start to gaze as if looking in the sky.
When night approaches he rolls up tight,
Until the morning when he finds the light.

Danie Price (11)
Holy Cross CE Junior School

Summer Flower

In my back garden I have a new fresh flower
It has lilac petals and a bright green stalk
with one leaf.
It looked very pretty
It stands out in the garden
and is the most beautiful flower anywhere.

Ellen Kerr (8)
Holy Cross CE Junior School

The Classroom Catastrophes

The mystical, magical Pritt stick pixie,
Short with a pointy hat,
Hovers at midnight with his friends,
And starts the toiling work.

The bold and bulky bags sit in rows of two,
They chat, mouths zipping, eyes flashing,
The animal coats scream like a zoo,
Then it's 3.30, time to go home.

The neglected and abandoned apparatus
Stands up tall, but bored,
His big red eyes brim with tears,
He suddenly yawns with a roar as children climb him.

The lovey-dovey salt and pepper are soulmates forever,
They got married yesterday.
The salt in her white dress and the pepper in his suit,
Although they look quite strange, they're actually quite clever!

The lonely, lost property box is lit up by the moonlight,
Full of food, yet she still gets more,
She feels all full and bloated,
She longs for love with all her might.

Tess Wauchope (11)
Holy Cross CE Junior School

My Dad

My dad gets up at 7 o'clock in the morning.
He gets dressed,
Gives me and Mummy a kiss and goes to work.
He gives me a kiss at night and tucks me up in bed.
Then my dad goes downstairs and watches TV with Mummy,
He talks to Mummy and has a peaceful time except
when I shout downstairs.

Eloise Sproul (7)
Holy Cross CE Junior School

A Journey Round Our School

The cowardly blinds smile uneasily,
As together they are slowly drawn,
They stand up aligned and towering,
Ready for a battle to commence once more at dawn.

The toilet's mouth is always open,
Waiting to be fed,
Waiting for the cleaning ladies
To come and put him to bed.

The piano never opens her mouth,
You have to find the right key,
If you don't she makes a din,
But she sings beautifully.

Salt and pepper dance together,
As tomato sauce sings,
The water jug rehydrates himself,
There's panic as the bell rings.

The photocopier whines,
As children push his buttons hard,
He longs to escape from this torture,
But he couldn't run a yard!

The radiator wails,'It's so hot,
I can't go on!' The radiator groans.
The caretaker comes to turn him off,
So no one can hear his moans!

Eloise Davies (11)
Holy Cross CE Junior School

Jasper

Jasper's my dog, he has a loud bark,
He loves big walks, down in the park,
Where he chases birds and runs away,
But he likes to play all day.

Jake Mullinder
Holy Cross CE Junior School

My Poem

The door sits there wide-eyed,
As he's shoved back and forth.
Suddenly he shouts out in pain,
As he's scraped across the floor.

As the piano hums his morning songs,
His insides working like the clappers.
But then the bell rings,
And once more he finds himself forlorn.

The sky-white ticking clock fearfully hides his face
Behind his spindly hands.
Perched there, nervously, as the grasping, prying human digits
Materialise before his quaking face.

The round, dusty bin squats beneath the desk,
Waiting patiently for his next meal of rubbish.
With his mouth wide open,
He stares longingly at the children making more mess.

Luke Wilde (11)
Holy Cross CE Junior School

Computer And Friends

The computer stands there like a tower chatting to his network friends,
He is always busy loading this and that.
The monitor girl stands with a screen, a lot of words and
                                        colours displaying.
The computer girl stands and shows off.
The mouse sits there like a hand waiting for a human
to come and move her around and click the button.
'Phew!' said the humans, 'these must get tired out!'

Nathan Morgan
Holy Cross CE Junior School

A Bad Morning

'You're late,' said Miss,
'The bell has rung,
Everyone's in class,
The assembly song has been sung,
And why is it that you're late?'
'Well, my sister's got the chickenpox,
My dad's got the flu,
My mum got stuck in a box,
I did too!
My brother tried to kill himself,
My sister's under stress,
My hamster fell off a shelf,
The house is now a mess.
My brother tried to hit me,
And I fell off my bike,
He was trying to tease me,
What am I like?'
'What are you like! Stop disturbing our class!'

Ellie Gough (9)
Holy Cross CE Junior School

The Moon Playing With The Ocean

The moon danced over the water,
Playing with the reflections, teasing,
Now you see me, now you don't.
The face of the moon, smiling
Down on the glittering waves and then
Hiding behind a cloud,
Suddenly frightened, before bravely stepping
Out to shine like a happy child, once
Again coming out to play.

Alex Collins (10)
Holy Cross CE Junior School

School Journey

The worthless, broken upset clock
Thinks she's been neglected.
She waves to everyone that passes,
Her problems aren't suspected.

The extremely tiny, brave mouse
Lies by the computer.
She's fed up of being picked up,
And she rides on a scooter.

The old tatty piano screams,
As the children press her high keys.
She decides not to open her mouth,
And she runs and hides behind trees.

The despondent bin groans miserably,
As children feed him food.
He only eats drink cartons,
And he's always in a mood.

The pillars stand up straight and tall,
They hold the ceiling high.
They wish they could all fly away,
And stay up in the sky.

The helpless, miserable, whiteboard whines,
As children rub out her face.
She starts to run but she's very slow,
And then she ends up in a cheerful place.

Lisa Bennett (11)
Holy Cross CE Junior School

Hot Yellow Sun

In the hot, bright, yellow sky,
Through the clouds, there was a hot bright light.
It was very shiny.
The sun disappeared, the rain came,
The clouds turned black as the sun went to sleep.

Fiona Jaynes (7)
Holy Cross CE Junior School

Personification

I stand alone on the shelf,
I am the pottery monk,
My legs stay here all day and night,
The night will give you quite a fright,
If you're standing next to me.

Who am I?
I'm the chair,
Because I'm always fit and fair,
Come and sit on my lap,
And give me a pat on the back.

I'm always on the wall,
Filling up with sound,
I say they're not allowed,
But they just totally ignore me,
As they fill my cheeks with sound.

I stand up day and night,
As people put my friends on me,
I always say,
'Why, oh why!'

I always sit on the wall,
I save your life,
As I shout, 'Fire! Fire!'
But I can shout louder than anyone.

How cool we are,
We're the knife and fork,
We hunt our prey,
But then humans take it off us,
Then our cool goes down.

The paper cutter is evil to me,
I'm Mr Paper,
It slices me and the gang in half,
But then there becomes more of us.

Why am I a pepper holder?
I'm always coughing,
Because of the stupid pepper,
So why am I a pepper holder?

Ben Woolley-Henfield (11)
Holy Cross CE Junior School

The Day School Came Alive

The chatterbox door has his conversation with the corridor
While people rumble through his territory
The murderer car-cutter kills his prey
With a slash of his fierce claw.

The brawny pegs support colossal coats
They tighten their grip and won't ever let go
At half-past three they drop their load
And take a rest until tomorrow.

The musical piano plays his song
And the children sing along
He is a delightful, lovely brown
But sometimes he wears a frown.

Ben Hadley (10)
Holy Cross CE Junior School

OHP

The OHP sits lonely and blue,
Waiting for someone who knows what to do.
Along comes a girl and presses his button,
'Eureka!' he cries, 'I've not been forgotten!'
He opens one eye, wide and bright,
His yawning mouth grins with delight.
The light from his belly shines up through the glass,
'Whooo!' he shouts, 'I'm top of the class!'

Conor Crozier (11)
Holy Cross CE Junior School

Personification

The outstretched, mucky floor longs to be remembered,
As children trample on his face,
And cleaners clean up his dirty nose,
But he just lies there silently, silently,
Hoping someone will remember, remember.

The whiteboard stands there all day long,
Lingering for someone to come along,
When the person comes, he stands up straight,
And when they're finished he'll wait and wait
For someone to come back with his baby,
Will anyone say 'thank you?' Maybe, maybe.

The sparkly, silver coat pegs are strong mums and sons,
As they chatter among them they wait for the bell to ring,
If you walk past them silently, you can hear the mums,
They give a sigh of relief when the bell goes ring, ring, ring.

The banner is the new guy,
He is the tallest, he can reach the sky,
He is so cool, he gets the most love,
And his girlfriend is a bright white dove.

The piano is a cheerful chap,
If you take off his hat there is a massive gap,
Some of his teeth are black and rotten,
He's used every day so he is not forgotten.

Salt and pepper are the best of mates,
They're two cheerful chaps that no one hates,
They are always together, you can't tell them apart,
They may be small but they both have a big heart.

The photocopier is a real funny guy,
When you walk past him you've got to say 'Hi!'
He will copy you until you cry,
And when you cry he'll give a sigh.

The card cutter is a mean old fellow,
Killing everything that gets in his way,
His favourite victim is card,
And that is how he got his mean old name.

Demi Lewendon & Amy Owen (11)
Holy Cross CE Junior School

Nonsense Animal Alphabet

The ache of an aardvark,
The bark of a bird.
The cry of a camel,
The dance of a damselfish.
The egg of an earthworm,
The fail of a falcon.
The gulp of a glow-worm,
The halt of a haddock.
The ingenuity of an iguana,
The jump of a jellyfish.
The kong of a kangaroo,
The laughter of a leech.
The magic of the monkey,
The noise of the nightingale.
The orange of the octopus,
The pounce of the panther.
The queue of the quails,
The run of the rabbits.
The star of the starfish,
The tantrum of a tiger.
The universe of sea-urchins,
The vanity of a viperfish.
The wail of a wallaby,
The x-factor of an x-ray fish.
The yahoo of a yak,
The zing of a zebra.

Annabel Minton (9)
Holy Cross CE Junior School

Star, Star

'Star, star, please come down to me,
I don't want to be alone,
That's why I want you to come down to me.'

'I will,' said the star,
'I will come down to you,
Watch me, I'm coming, I'm coming down to you.'

So the star went down, then went up,
She never saw it again, again, again,
She never saw it again.

Lucy Cole (8)
Holy Cross CE Junior School

My Brother

My brother has spiky hair,
He looks like a koala bear.

He's tall and thin,
And has hairs on his chin.

He plays the guitar,
But can't drive a car.

George Hughes (7)
Holy Cross CE Junior School

Friday

F riday comes once a week,
R eally excited about Friday,
I like Friday, it's the best
D ay at school, but Saturday's next,
A day to have some fun,
Y ahoo! It's Friday.

Evie Cartwright (9)
Longden CE Primary School

The Goblin Band

In a faraway land,
There was a really cool band,
They were called The Goblins,
They went to Dublin.

They did a very good song,
And it was very long,
They sang
And it ended with a bang.

The Goblins were number one,
They went to the prom
To play their song
And did it wrong.

First there were nine
Then there were five
Then there was one
And then they were gone.

Callum Murtha (11)
Longden CE Primary School

The Bin Monster

Once upon a rhyme,
In a very great time,
There lived a monster,
Who was called Ronster.

The great thing about him
Was he lived in a bin,
Until the binman came along,
And chucked him in with the awful pong.

He had a big belly,
Full of jelly,
He was very fat,
Until he went *splat*.

Craig Davies (11)
Longden CE Primary School

Greek Gods

Zeus and Hera,
King and queen,
To each other they could be
Rather mean.

Athena and Ares,
Jealous, always,
Their fighting could go on
For days and days.

Artemis and Apollo,
Both with archery skill,
With bow and arrow
They both would not wound, but kill.

Hades and Persephone,
They rule the underworld,
Their undead flag
Unfurled.

All these gods and more,
There certainly weren't a few,
Like a big family they were
They didn't half argue!

James Pereira (11)
Longden CE Primary School

My Friend Is . . .

M y friend is . . .
Y oung and pretty,

F ragile and feminine,
R eliable and kind,
I s fun,
E verything you can think of,
N ice and friendly,
D aft and silly.

Gail Butler (10)
Longden CE Primary School

Overrun

One Monday in the month of May
A baker set out to work for the day,
He baked fresh bread and lots of sugared buns
To fill all the children's empty tums.

But round about noon as the bread began to steam
In crept a little fiend,
His eyes were like olives, his feet and tail were pink
And he never even stopped to have a think.

Gradually more and more came creeping through the hole in the door,
The scent of buns drawing them near as they crept across the floor,
Then they were upon the food nibbling away,
The baker came in and his face turned grey.

'Out! Out! he cried, and ran at the breads,
The friends scattered and crammed through the hole bumping and
                                          shoving their heads.
They ran out into the street,
'Oh no, they've had the food, there's nothing left to eat!'

Kate Nixon (11)
Longden CE Primary School

I've Been Here

I've been to a place way up high
In a hot air balloon in the sky.

I've been to a place way down low
At the bottom of the sea where the octopus go.

I've been to a place in outer space
There an alien asked me for a race.

I've been to a place where it's very hot
I liked it there quite a lot.

I've been to places here and there,
What to do next, I can't think where.

Lucy Fotheringham (9)
Longden CE Primary School

Little Red Riding Hood

A little girl went through a wood,
Her name was Little Red Riding Hood.

She came out of her home with a basket of food,
Then she was in a very happy mood.

A wolf followed her down the path,
Little Red Riding Hood said, 'Pooh! Haven't you had a bath?'

The wolf exclaimed with a frown,
'I'll chase that girl into town!

Where are you going?' said the wolf one day,
'To my granny's,' Little Red Riding Hood said as she began to pray.

She prayed that he wouldn't chase her,
With his big sharp teeth and straggly fur.

The wolf ran ahead to Granny's house,
He ran fast and quietly like a mouse.

He got into bed and dressed up like Granny,
Locked Granny in the cupboard, poor nanny.
When Little Red Riding Hood came along,
She scared the wolf away with a terrible song.

Emma Greig (10)
Longden CE Primary School

My Family

My family are . . .
Young and old.

Funny and friendly
And they are very kind, considerate,
My family are the best, but sometimes they are pests.
I love my family because they are
Loving, caring,
You can't get a family as nice as mine.

Andrew Rotchell (10)
Longden CE Primary School

My Beach

Up on a cliff top,
a beach down below.
How do you get there?
I really don't know.
Find a secret passageway,
Where does it lead?
No signs to follow,
No maps to read.
Two passageways,
which one shall I take?
I can't see anything
it could lead to a lake.
Finally I see a bit of golden brown,
my peaceful beach has been found,
resting after that long walk,
I will come back tomorrow,
I will come back for more.

Rebecca Griffiths (10)
Longden CE Primary School

In The Garden

In the garden we have fifteen tulips,
No cauliflower.

The daffodils are growing fast,
Heaps of daisies,
Enormous amounts of sunflowers.

Great big dock leaves,
And lots of bluebells.
Roses smell great.
Do come,
Especially to see the lilies.

Lucy Lewis (9)
Longden CE Primary School

Beauty Sleep

In a castle
Far, far away,
Slept Sleeping Beauty
Until this day.

Around the castle
Men did creep,
To knock it down
And disturb her sleep.

Trying to knock down the wall,
Trying to break down the door,
Got through the roof,
Seeing her they fell to the floor.

Cleared the cobwebs
From her face,
Touching her cheeks
With tender grace.

And kissed her lips
The most gentle and kindly
The first word she said
For a hundred years - 'Finally!'

Emily Cox (10)
Longden CE Primary School

Black Flames

Black flames with an icy glimmer create death,
Black flames take your soul for a toll,
Black flames burn the living,
Black flames make the soul quiver and twist your liver,
Black flames torture you to your death.
Black flames always remain and can't be trained,
Black flames will live for ever.

This is a warning, remember this for ever.

Alaister Watkins (10)
Longden CE Primary School

Animal Alphabet

A is for ant, who is very tiny,
B is for bat, who flies very well,
C is for cat, who has lots of naps,
D is for dog, who does loads of laps,
E is for eel, who swims all around,
F is for fish, who have scales everywhere,
G is for giraffe, who is very tall,
H is for horse, who gallops around,
I is for iguana, who is a lizard,
J is for jellyfish, who is like a bubble,
K is for koala, who likes to eat leaves,
L is for lion, who is the king of the jungle,
M is for monkey, who is very cheeky,
N is for newts who are like frogs,
O is for octopus who has lots of legs,
P is for pig, who likes mud,
Q is for quail, who gets eaten by whales,
R is for rabbit, who is very jumpy,
S is for snake, who is very scary,
T is for turtle, who is very slow,
U is for umbrella birds who are very good singers,
V is for vulture who is a meat eater,
W is for whale, who whistles,
X is for X-ray fish, who glows,
Y is for yak who is very hairy,
Z is for zebra, who is very stripy.

Josie Murtha (9)
Longden CE Primary School

Starlit Towns

Empty darkness on
Towns, starlit night, jagged
Light, bright, icy stars.

Scott Dixon (11)
Longden CE Primary School

The 3 Crafty Pigs

There once were 3 little pigs,
Bob, Charlie and Digs.
Bob built his house out of bricks,
But Wolf came with his tricks.
Wolf said, 'Little pig, please let me in
Or I'll get a bulldozer and knock your house in.'
'No, please don't, I'm only a pig with a little pink chin.'
But he got his bulldozer and knocked his house in.

There once were 3 little pigs,
Bob, Charlie and Digs.
Charlie built his house out of stone,
And Wolf came with a moan.
Wolf said, 'Little pig, please let me in
Or I'll get a bulldozer and knock your house in.'
'No, please don't, I'm only a pig with a little pink chin.'
But he got his bulldozer and knocked his house in.

There were once 3 little pigs
Bob, Charlie and Digs.
Digs built his house out of wood,
But Wolf came with his friend and stood.
Wolf said, 'Little pig please let me in
Or I'll get a bulldozer and knock your house in.
But Digs filled his house with explosives and said, 'Come in,'
He rain out the back way and waited for a *'Hey,'*
Followed by a *bang!*

Oliver Emery (11)
Longden CE Primary School

Spring Mornings Haiku

Clear spring morning air,
Bees buzz around, birds sing loud.
The cuckoo calls out.

Katy Jones (10)
Longden CE Primary School

The Big Bad Wolf

There once were three little pigs
Who all left home at six,
The house was too full,
Their mum had to be strong
To say goodbye to her children.

Once there was a little girl called Red
Who was definitely properly fed,
She went to her gran's
But a wolf was her nan,
But she was saved by a very old man.

Now this wolf that tried to eat Miss Hood
Was really not very good,
He tried to get the three pigs
Because he hoped they would taste of figs.
The wolf was bad,
He was definitely mad
But he always tried his best.

Georgina Davies (10)
Longden CE Primary School

Haiku

The night ends as the
Sun comes out, animals run
Awake, free till dusk.

Cerian Abbott (10)
Longden CE Primary School

Winter Frozen Haiku

Moon clear and dark sky.
Darkness creeps, foxes stumble.
All on a cold night.

Lucy Hickson (10)
Longden CE Primary School

The Magician's Handbook

In the magician's handbook
are kept thousands of notes
things like how to turn four cockroaches into five goats.

In the magician's handbook
are kept mysterious things
like how to turn pebbles into diamond rings.

In the magician's handbook
are kept far-off lands
like underwater villages and desert sands.

In the magician's handbook
are kept wonderful potions
like gold mixtures and death curing lotions.

In the magician's handbook
are kept many of these chants
like how to put friends into an eerie trance.

Sam W Rintoul (9)
Longden CE Primary School

The Monsters

Once there was a little goblin who always told jokes,
And then there was a big giant who picked on old folks.

Once there was a tiny dragon who stayed under a bridge,
And then there was a monster who lived in a large fridge.

Once there was a big gremlin who was green and tall,
And then there was Humpty Dumpty who was much like a ball.

Once there was a large fairy who always played tig,
And then there was a gnome who used to wear a wig.

Once there was an average ogre who had a big belly,
And then there was an orc who used to eat jelly.

Once there were three big bears who ate some foxes,
And then there were lots of wolves who stayed in boxes.

Laura Price (9)
Longden CE Primary School

Robin Hood

Robin Hood is very good
In the trees of Sherwood,
Takes from the greedy, gives to the needy,
In the trees of Sherwood.
His merry men are in their den
In the trees of Sherwood.
When they are eating,
Robin's creeping
Through the trees of Sherwood.
And Little John, his arrows gone,
In the trees of Sherwood,
The army die as arrows fly
In the trees of Sherwood.
And legend says in the old days they lived
In the trees of Sherwood.

James Rowson (10)
Longden CE Primary School

The Dragon

In the cave
There's a dragon,
He breathes out fire like a wave,
With his sharp teeth and claws.

All around the story spreads,
About the dragon in the mountain,
Most of the rumours are that he'll grind your bones for his bread,
But you know, that's what giants do.

People all around try to slay him,
To try and save the princess,
But she tears them up from limb to limb,
What they don't know is there's nothing to save.

Maddy Cartwright (11)
Longden CE Primary School

Winter

Crunchy, white, cold snow,
Flowing streams covered in ice
In the winter nights.

Frozen icicles
Hanging from the ice-cold sky
With shimmering stars.

Blue frost-bites fingers
Making snowmen and snowballs
That gradually melt.

Laura Wallen (10)
Longden CE Primary School

Can I Have?

Can I have a flying pig?
Can I have a boy called Matt?
Can I have a diving cow?
Can I have a gold tabby cat?

Can I have a singing bird?
Can I have a diamond ring?
Can I have a fluffy chicken?
Can I have a long spring?

Can I have a boring kiddie?
Can I have some howling dogs?
Can I have a crying baby?
Can I have some soggy Kellogg's?

Can I have?
Can I have?
Can I have
Everything?

Abigail Louise Evans (8)
Longlands Primary School

The Rhinoceros

The king of the forest
Lumbering through the soft breeze
Powerful charger
Dangerous hunter
Headbutter
A tank with legs
Where are you now?

Where is the sweet sound of the rhino's call?
Sold for a teaspoon of medicine.
This strong animal, helpless to a rifle,
The animal whose life has just begun
Fell swiftly to the ground
At the sound of a gun.

Jonathan Harrison (11)
Longlands Primary School

The Writer Of This Poem
(Based on 'The Writer Of This Poem' by Roger McGough)

The writer of this poem
Is taller than a house,
As keen as a king,
As handsome as my mum.

As bold as a boxing glove,
As sharp as a knife,
As strong as a brick,
As tricky as a fib.

As smooth as an ice lolly,
As quick as a lick,
As clean as a chemist's shop,
As clever as a tick.

Rebecca Jane Parton (11)
Longlands Primary School

Who Am I?

Its mouth is a volcano
Just like a sauna, all bubbly and brave,
A bottomless pit in a cave.
Its tongue is a flag ready to flicker,
Like orange peel, all scaly and bitter.
Its evil eyes are burning lava,
Its smoking snout red and gold,
In with the new year, out with the old.

A bulging sunset of colour
Getting ready to pounce,
A mix of sugar and spice,
Feet dancing to the beat,
The tail goes swaying through the street,
A fiery giant
Twirling, swirling, whirling into the darkness.

Who am I?
Well, can't you guess?
I'm the Chinese Dragon
From the east.

Millie Thomas (11)
Longlands Primary School

Snow

I went to school this morning feeling rather sad,
And when I got into the classroom, it was really mad.

Snow is falling on my head as well as on my class,
Snow is falling on the trees and also on the grass.

Snow will never end as long as we live,
Snow is the best thing that God could give.

Lauren Williams (8)
Longlands Primary School

Let Me . . .

Let me go to school,
Let me swim in the pool,
Let me learn my times tables,
Let me work it out.

Let me draw a picture,
Let me paint the trees,
Let me paint the sky all blue,
Let me paint the ground.

Let me in the hall,
Let me play with my old ball,
Let me shine the windows,
Let me sing aloud.

Let me do the alphabet,
Let me spell my words,
Let me pick the paper up,
Let me stamp on the floor.

Courtney Duce (9)
Longlands Primary School

In My Room

There's a monster in my bedroom, Mum,
I'll tell you what it's like.
Its head is like a dog ready to fight,
Its body is like a slippy, slimy snake,
Its claws are like my sister with her red, sharp nails,
Its teeth are like scissors getting ready to snip.
I know you don't believe me Mum, but hurry it's getting closer,
It . . . *aarrggh!*

Ainsley Almond (11)
Longlands Primary School

The Chinese Dragon

Dancing through the cheering street
With its stamping rounded feet,
Shimmering golden eyes
Flickering like fire,
The brightness makes my eyes tire.

Clinging claws,
Snapping jaws,
Snout smoking like a chimney,
All I can hear is millions of cheers
Popping both my ears.

Flakey scales,
Waving tail,
Pointed, daggered teeth,
Swaying to the beat,
Dancing in the street.

Camilla Anne Edwards (10)
Longlands Primary School

Elephant

There's an elephant in Africa
With a very swishy tail,
His name is Jacob Joe
And he always used to fail.
Whenever he tried to do something,
All his friends would laugh,
So in the end he decided
To go off with his friend, the giraffe.

Dominic Sheridan (8)
Longlands Primary School

King Of The Jungle

King of Africa,
Brave as can be,
Can you see him?
Where can he be?

King of Africa,
Can you see
An animal prowling
Through the trees?

King of Africa,
Where are you now?
Behind the trees, ready to pounce?
No you're on an office floor
To be walked on for evermore.

Sarah Butter (11)
Longlands Primary School

Lord Of Africa

Elephant so dangerous,
tree trunk legs,
boulder built body,
enormous floppy ears,
nose swaying in the breezy air,
tusk is guarding himself.
Mammoth.

Innocent, gentle giant,
never attacks unless
threatened!

Where are you now?
Gone for ever
after the sound of a gun!

Elliott Bennett (10)
Longlands Primary School

The Animal Bus Poem

20 bats living in the boot,
19 lions living on the top,
18 ducks flying in the bus,
17 scorpions living in the pipes,
16 eagles looking out on top,
15 wombats eating all the food,
14 tortoises that eat all the trees,
13 hamsters that eat all the peanuts,
12 dogs barking at the ducks,
11 cats chasing all the eagles,
10 dragons killing all the people,
9 snakes helping all the dragons,
8 slugs slurping and burping,
7 worms fighting with the slugs,
6 kangaroos kickboxing each other,
5 monkeys jumping around the bus,
4 cows drinking all the milk,
3 pigs eating all the pork,
2 rats eating the chairs,
1 rabbit fighting with the wombat, and
0 humans after the bomb was dropped.

Paul K Clarke (9)
Longlands Primary School

Lion, Lion

Lion, lion, deadly but beautiful,
How do you do it?
Lion, lion, really deadly
When you are stalking your prey.
Lion, lion so fast
We can't even see your beauty.

Jeffrey Pollard (8)
Longlands Primary School

At The Zoo

I went to the zoo on a very sunny day,
Went into the restaurant to have a big buffet.
As soon as I sat down I saw something moving,
It was a little monkey doing the hoovering.

I thought I was dreaming, but it turned out I was not,
I chased him out the door, he was going like a shot!
He ran into his cage and shut the door tight,
Then I shouted for the keeper which I thought was right.

I saw the keeper coming, his face was very red,
I looked at the monkey that was sleeping on his bed.
When I saw the monkey still sleeping on his bed,
Then he started snoring which went round and round my head.

I went back into the restaurant, my mum and dad weren't there,
I looked all around and found them at the fair,
I went to get some candyfloss and went on a ride,
And then I caught my mum and dad, they were trying to hide.
That was my day at the zoo but on the way back I needed the loo!

Bethany Cash (8)
Longlands Primary School

Zebras

Zebras, zebras
You are black and white.
You gallop across the plain so fast
We cannot see your stripes.
When you're thirsty
You stop by a river and take a sip of water
Then you are off again.
When you are sleepy
You lie in the grass,
Your tail swishing from side to side.

Leigh Edwards (8)
Longlands Primary School

Let Me . . .

Let me go to school,
Let me swim in the pool,
Let me have a cat,
Let me play with the bat.

Let me put my work on the table,
Let me pull the cable,
Let me get rid of the pond,
Let me have a video of James Bond.

Let me go in the hall,
Let me play with my ball,
Let me draw a dot,
Let me put my doll in the baby's cot.

Let me pick,
Let me have that stick,
Let me go to bed,
Let me break the lead.

Stacey Bradshaw (9)
Longlands Primary School

Tyler's Pets

Ten penguins that live in the freezer,
Nine lions that sleep all day,
Eight scorpions that lie in the bed,
Seven dragons lie in a wardrobe,
Six slugs that crawl on the walls,
Five tiger sharks that live in the bath,
Four hamsters that lie in the pants' drawer,
Three pigs that eat all the food,
Two hairy tarantulas that go in your hair,
One guess what?

Tyler Crump (8)
Longlands Primary School

Alphabet Poem

A is for Adam who eats a lot of curry,
B is for Beth who can do cartwheels,
C is for Chris who left in a hurry,
D is for Danny who never kneels
E is for Elizabeth who likes ants,
F is for Fred who picks his nose,
G is for Gregory who dirties his pants,
H is for Harry who wets everyone with a hose,
I is for Ivy who is always bored,
J is for Jake who likes races,
K is for Katie who has an award,
L is for Laura who has 6 races,
M is for Mr Nodder who is cuddly,
N is for Nancy who hates everyone,
O is for Olly who fancies Lea,
P is for Polly who can't count to twenty-one.
Q is for Queen who nicks bits and bobs,
R is for Robert who hates me,
S is for Sally who sings the hits,
T is for Tom who loves the sea,
U is for Unity who eats a lot of meat,
V is for Vanessa who is my sister,
W is for Will who likes the heat,
X is for X-Y who hates her,
Y is for Yobby who eats veg,
Z is for Zeo who fell off a ledge.

Andrew Blake (9)
Longlands Primary School

Poem . . . ?

A is for Abbey who is mad,
B is for Beth who is bad,
C is for Chelsea who is terribly boring,
D is for Declan who is naughty,
E is for Elizabeth who is mad,
F is for Fred who is happy,
G is for Greg who has left the class,
H is for Harry who is bad,
I is for Ivy who is a fusser
J is for Jade who is noisy,
K is for Katie who is bad,
L is for Laura who is happy,
M is for Megan who is sad,
N is for Natasha who is a silly billy,
O is for octopus swimming in the sea,
P is for Paul who is happy,
Q is for Queen who is generous,
R is for Robert who is a bully,
S is for Sophie who is cheeky,
T is for Tracey who is happy,
U is for Uncle who makes a noise,
V is for Vicky who makes a mess,
W is for William who is sad,
X is for X-ray which scares me,
Y is for yo-yo which goes up and down,
Z is for zoo with animals.

Katie Dykes (9)
Longlands Primary School

Alphabet

A is for Abby who is terribly mad,
B is for bird which sings in the tree,
C is for Courtney who is crazy,
D is for Darren who is bad,
E is for elephant which drinks with his trunk,
F is for Fred who is sad,
G is for Greg who is naughty,
H is for Harry who is stupid,
I is for Ivy who is a pain in the bum,
J is for Jasmine who is terribly nasty,
K is for Katie who is terribly boring,
L is for Laura who is happy,
M is for Matthew who is noisy,
N is for Natasha who is a bully,
O is for octopus which swims in the sea,
P is for Paul who is nasty
Q is for Queen who is generous,
R is for Ryan who is sad,
S is for Sophie and I don't know why,
T is for Tracy who sucks her thumb,
U is for Uncle who plays with me,
V is for Vicky who is terribly happy,
W is for William who is very, very sad,
X is for X-ray which shocks me out,
Y is for yo-yo which bounces,
Z is for zoo which makes loads of noise.

Chelsea Louise Barber (8)
Longlands Primary School

My Poem

A is for apple that makes a crunch,
B is for banana that you can munch,
C is for cats that can never be in a bunch,
D is for demon that comes around in the night,
E is for elephant that's a terrible sight,
F is for fish that can do a flip,
G is for goat that can dip,
H is for hat that you can wear,
I is for igloo, so take care,
J is for jelly that wiggles,
K is for kite that squiggles
L is for lemon that is very strong,
M is for mouse that has a long tongue,
N is for noisy that we are not now,
O is for octopus that has eight legs, but how,
P is for people that we are,
Q is for queen who likes jam,
R is for rabbit that bounces around,
S is for Siân that plays on the playground,
T is for tree that has a long trunk,
U is for umbrella that has a bump,
V is for violin that I don't play,
W is for wet, and please don't stay,
X is for X-ray that I really hate,
Y is for yo-yo that spins round and round,
Z is for zebra that makes a sound.

Jasmine Humphrey (8)
Longlands Primary School

Gentle Nights

Washing down the hills,
Waving through the leaves that are
Whistling round and round in circles
Again and again.
Winding the birds that are flying home.
Whooshing me against the wall.

Vanessa Blake **(7)**
Longlands Primary School

Gentle Wind

Whistling through the mountains,
Whispering in the trees.
Winding round the treetops,
Waving to me.
Washing through the darkness
And through the feelings of me.

Emma Henderson **(7)**
Longlands Primary School

I Went To School And What Did I See?

I went to school and what did I see?
I saw a teacher who looked at me.

I went to school and what did I see?
I saw a picture staring at me.

I went to school and what did I see?
I saw my friend smiling at me.

Kieron Evans **(7)**
Longlands Primary School

Rover Poem

Down among the dustbins
I met a dog called Rover,
She's such a stinky show-off though,
I wish today was over.
'No I need something better for a Rover poem.'
'OK.'
Down behind the dustbins
I met a dog called Rover,
She's such a mighty megastar,
I called her Supernova.
'Supernova, what a name to call a dog,
Can you do another one, please?'
'OK.'
Down behind the dustbins
I met a dog called Rover,
I thought that school might cure her,
But she took the whole place over.

Taylor Page (9)
Myddle CE Primary School

Teddy

Field racer
squirrel chaser.

Loud howler
big growler.

Big nose,
smelly toes.

Whippy tail,
flash of hail:

My greyhound, Teddy.

Marie Teleki (11)
Myddle CE Primary School

Seasons

Spring's here,
April showers,
Trees in bud,
Pots of flowers.

Summer's here,
All is bright,
Flowers in bloom,
What a sight.

Autumn's here,
The leaves float down,
Dew on cobwebs,
A colourful ground.

Winter's here,
Trees are bare,
Snow is falling
Everywhere.

Devan Morgan (10)
Myddle CE Primary School

The Song Of The Drunken Musician

Hubble bubble, toil and trouble,
Fire burn and cauldron bubble.
Note of guitar, string of violin,
Piece of piano and a bottle of gin!

Hubble bubble, toil and trouble,
Fire burn and cauldron bubble.
Whistle of flute, bang of drum,
Blow of saxophone and a chew of gum.

Hubble bubble toil and trouble,
Fire burn and cauldron bubble.

Emily Abrahams (9)
Myddle CE Primary School

Kennings Cat

Milk-drinker
Mouse-chaser
Day-sleeper
Person-scratcher
Happy-purrer
Food-eater
Scratch-player
Good-hider
Tree-climber
Drawer-sleeper.

Zoe Croft (9)
Myddle CE Primary School

Kennings Cat

Tail-wagger
Cat-sniffer
Long-whiskers
Short-legs
Loud-purr
Long-claws
Moon-watcher
Dog-chaser
Mice-eater
Eye-reflector
Long-sleeper
Milk-licker.

Delphine Price (9)
Myddle CE Primary School

Thy Yonder Castle

See thy yonder castle,
thy lighted castle,
'tis lighted by a mighty dragon
but thy dragon guards a
maiden fair
with hair of gold
but face of cold
because thy dragon keeps thy
knights away.
None to save her,
thy maiden fair
in thy yonder castle,
thy lighted castle.

Nathan Kavanagh (10)
Myddle CE Primary School

Weird Thoughts

One night I was lying in my bed,
Weird thoughts came crashing through my head.
What if a dragon came for tea?
What if the tea was really me?
Stop! These thoughts they are so strange,
Monsters chewing up my brains!
I must realise that I am here,
Safe from harm - nothing to fear.
(Except my brother -
He's really scary!)

Holly Steed (10)
Myddle CE Primary School

Your Faithful Friend

Y our faithful friend,
O ur friendship will never end,
U nderstanding and caring,
R eally kind and sharing.

F aithful friend who will always be there,
A lways loving,
I love being around my faithful friend,
T elling each other our secrets,
H onest and loving,
F un to play with,
U ntruthful never,
L ovely smile every day.

F orgiving always,
R ing her every single day,
I n a good mood for ever,
E xcellent friend you make,
N othing will break you apart,
D oing favours for each other.

Laura Urbano (10)
Our Lady & St Oswald's Catholic Primary School

A Poem For Christmas

Smelly cheese,
Christmas trees,

Lots of Christmas spirit.

Snowflakes falling,
People calling.

Lots of Christmas spirit.

Eating pies,
Starry skies.

Ideal Christmas spirit.

Rachael Holbrook (7)
Our Lady & St Oswald's Catholic Primary School

I Wish

If I could have a wish
I would wish for
A holiday in Australia.
To become a lion cub
To even meet an alien,
To never drink in a pub.

If I could have a wish,
My wish would be
To have a little puppy.
Go all around the Earth,
To be very lucky,
To know a little Smurf.

If I could have a wish
That little wish would be
To not have to go to school.
To get a birthstone ring,
To have my own swimming pool,
To even meet the future king.

Lucy Hibbitt (10)
Our Lady & St Oswald's Catholic Primary School

What I Want

I want a car, big and green,
I want to move out when I'm eighteen.
I want a mansion, big and roomy,
I want to run the marathon, nice and smoothly.
I want a tour guide to show me beautiful sights,
I want to have dreams every single night.
I want to climb a mountain that is an enormous height,
I want to sleep peacefully every single night.
But all I really want is to be me,
That is what I really want to see.

Sebastian Pierpoint (8)
Our Lady & St Oswald's Catholic Primary School

An Air Raid In The Second World War

The bombs are exploding,
People are screaming,
Death is streaming
All over London.

Brother is frightened,
Mother is scared,
People are terrified,
All over London.

The smell is choking,
The taste of dust,
The view is devastating,
All over London.

The touch of the ashes,
Once the planes have gone,
The weeping of people
All over London.

Another day passes,
The bombers return,
Along with fear lurking,
All over London.

Frances Carrasco (11)
Our Lady & St Oswald's Catholic Primary School

Dolphin

D olphins are so very graceful,
O utstanding in their appearance as they swim about,
L eaping in and out of the water.
P laying in the oceans
H igh in the air they fly,
I n and out of the waves,
N othing looks as wonderful.

Harriet Strefford (11)
Our Lady & St Oswald's Catholic Primary School

Spring

Spring
Spring is a time when leaves grow,
And when the new lambs wear a bow.
Spring is a time when birds sing,
Beautiful songs, sun on their wings.

Spring
Flowers in bud, ready to grow,
Farmers are busy ready to sow.
Bluebells make a blanket blue
Trees are sprouting, leaves anew.

Spring
Sunny days and frequent showers,
Warmth and drink for hungry flowers.
All these things God will bring,
How we thank the Lord for spring.

Rebecca Jones (9)
Our Lady & St Oswald's Catholic Primary School

My Best Friend

When my best friend comes to play
We seem to giggle most of the day
We disappear into my room
But all she talks about is Orlando Bloom
She loved the film 'Lord Of The Rings;
But I wish she'd talk about other things
We both like swimming in the pool
It's so much better than going to school
She always does well in work and tests
And always tries her very best
She's gentle and kind and never fights
Even in the dead of night
She's nice and kind and makes me smile
I'll hope we'll be friends for a long, long while.

Natalie Renwick (9)
Our Lady & St Oswald's Catholic Primary School

Night

I saw at dusk
The face of night,
Fragile, fair and motionless.

Her dress of silk,
Spider's web is sow,
From a desolate cave
I hear her moan.

She glides upon the hills at night,
Silent is she,
As she comes in sight.

Night's mystical air
And harmonious feel,
Makes your dreams seem so unreal.

So silent is night,
She silently slips
Out of our mind with her hand on her lips.

Till dawn arrives, she by our side
As we wake up
She goes to hide.

A howling wind
Across the sky,
There she hides till day is nigh.

Rebecca Ozanne (10)
Our Lady & St Oswald's Catholic Primary School

Dragons

A dry hiss
The scrape of a claw,
You try to see what it is once more,
But no one can tell who owns the black wings.

It moves into the light
And there you see
A dragon looking straight back at me
With its dinner-plate eyes.

A scream and a roar,
You stumble and fall.
A talon you feel on your wrist
Then the clock starts to chime.

Tick-tock, tick-tock,
The time growing ever nearer,
Tick-tock, one o'clock!
All dragons must hide away.

Dragon hunting isn't fun,
On a cold winter night.
I'd much rather cuddle up in bed
But it's always good to try something new!

Sarah Coxhead (10)
Our Lady & St Oswald's Catholic Primary School

Dreams

I dreamt I was a goldfish
Swimming in a bowl
But in fact when I woke up
I was a garden mole.

I dreamt I was a rainbow
Stretching across the sky
But in fact when I woke up
I was a meatball in a pie.

I dreamt I was some glasses
Sitting on a nose
But in fact when I woke up
I was someone's wriggly toes.

I dreamt I was a flower
Dancing in the breeze
But in fact when I woke up
I was an acorn in the trees.

Amy Jones (9)
Our Lady & St Oswald's Catholic Primary School

Magic Box

(Based on 'Magic Box' by Kit Wright)

I will put in my magic box . . .

A claw from the tamest tiger
A horn from the whitest unicorn
A feather from the largest eagle

I will put in my magic box . . .

A smile from a newborn baby
A gallop from the fastest horse
A jump from the craziest kangaroo.

Isabelle Makin (8)
Our Lady & St Oswald's Catholic Primary School

A Friend In Me

I have a friend
She's in a place no one can see

She's always there for me
She helps me when I'm down
She's always kind and helpful
But never has a frown

She's always there for me
She flies like an angel
Soars around in the sky
And even though I cannot see
I'll always love the friend in me!

Zoë Davies (9)
Our Lady & St Oswald's Catholic Primary School

Dolphins

Dolphins are playful
They swim in the blue
They are so playful
They like to swim with you

When the sun goes down
And the moon comes up
The ocean is theirs
Oh, to have no cares

When the sun glistens on the sea
I know they're waiting patiently
For the squeals of delight to fill the air
From children and adults who come to stare.

Bethany Griffiths (8)
Our Lady & St Oswald's Catholic Primary School

Chickens

Chickens are very lively animals,
always trying to fly out of their pens.
They are black and white, brown and white and some are dark red.
They lay fresh brown speckled eggs especially
for cooked breakfast especially with
bacon, sausages, chips and fried tomato.
They have a little red wavy comb on top of
their heads which is very bendy.
Chickens like fresh water and fresh layer pellets.
At night when they go to sleep they climb on
top of their perch and shut their eyes.
They are also good for security when they cluck.
When you go to collect the eggs
they stamp in the water to splash you.
The chicken family is a rooster's best friend
cluck, cluck, cluck, cluck!
It's chickens!

Ashley Davies (9)
Our Lady & St Oswald's Catholic Primary School

September

September when autumn is coming,
September when the nights draw in.
September when the leaves start to fall.

September when it might be sunny
September when our birthdays might be.
September time for the harvest.

September when school starts again,
September when we re-meet teachers and school friends
September when summer ends.

Rosie Keaney (10)
Our Lady & St Oswald's Catholic Primary School

I Have A Guinea Pig

I have a guinea pig in me
It scratches and scrambles
It runs and rambles
It's mad and moody
It's still and silent
It's lost and lonely
It's crazy and caring
It's playful and patient
It's fab and furry
It's happy and hungry
It's cheeky and chirpy
And I love him.

Emily Bound (9)
Our Lady & St Oswald's Catholic Primary School

Chocolate

Chocolate is yummy
And very, very scrummy.
It makes me scream,
Oh chocolate's my dream!
Sweetly the chocolate smelt
As the warm air made it melt.
There's dark and there's white,
You can even buy 'light'.
For chocolate is yummy
As it goes in my tummy.
Most girls like Twirls,
Most boys prefer toys.

Emma Harding (10)
Our Lady & St Oswald's Catholic Primary School

Winter In The Woods

The year is coming to an end,
The big blue sky is getting colder.
Evenings are drawing in.
The nights are clear and out in the woods the
Wolf howls to the full moon.

Animals are hibernating,
Snowflakes fall to the ground.
The grass is as white as snow.
Icicles hang, misty and mysterious, on the branches
Of the trees as the moon casts its shadow.

A barn owl sits in the tree looking for his supper,
A badger scurries into his set.
A fox creeps silently through the snow, leaving
Only his footprints, in the light of the silvery moon.

Night draws to a close,
Daylight begins to break,
Morning is nigh.
The hungry robin pecks for worms in the cold
Hard Earth, as the birds begin their daylight chorus.

Winter is here.

Ebony Clay (9)
Our Lady & St Oswald's Catholic Primary School

The Boogly Woogly Bear

As fast as a cheetah
But smaller than a mouse,
With a big long trunk
And a tiny, whiny mouth.

With dotted skin
With a huge black nose,
And wears a fluffy hat
That's as white as a rose.

It crawls round the fireplace
And when the flames are on
It grows to two centimetres
But always goes back to one.

As I walk past his shelter,
I give a little wave.
He sort of smiles at me
In a friendly sort of way.

I didn't know what he was,
And I didn't know his name.
So I called him the Boogly Woogly Bear,
All cuddly, loveable and tame.

Rhianna Carrasco (9)
Our Lady & St Oswald's Catholic Primary School

When I Grow Up

When I grow up I want to be a pro surfer.
I want to ride the thumping breakers,
To swim the deep blue
And see the fish so colourful and bright.
That makes me feel alone and free.

When I grow up I want to be a famous diver,
Exploring wrecks beneath the sea
And finding treasure with oh such pleasure.
But it might not happen to me . . .

Oh what a life under the sea.

When I grow up I want to be a skateboarder
And ride the concrete waves.
Like diving in the clouds so white,
To ollie in the air so fresh and bright.

When I grow up, my name will still be Hollie,
But through all that -
I still can't ollie.
Oh my golly!

(Ollie is a skating jump)

Hollie Jones (9)
Our Lady & St Oswald's Catholic Primary School

Agitating Adults

Why do grown-ups say daft things?
I'm blessed if I should know.
Some nights when I'm wide awake
They say, 'Off to bed you go.'

Yet when I'm fast asleep,
All comfy in my sheet,
They talk in very loud voices
And start irritating my feet.

At breakfast it's the same,
'You must tidy up.'
I moan and grown and say,
'Only the cup!'

I hope that when I'm older
I don't repeat those lines.
But if I forget,
It was their fault, not mine.

Natalie Jones (9)
Our Lady & St Oswald's Catholic Primary School

Have You Ever Seen?

Have you ever seen a joker juggling with ice cream
Or a pair of giant hamsters, wrestling in your dreams?
Have you ever eaten twenty conkers?
Then you my friend, are totally and utterly bonkers!

Have you ever seen a jellyfish climb up a wall,
Or a caterpillar who plays football?
Have you ever seen an elephant sit on a dairy?
Then you my friend, are totally and utterly crazy!

Have you ever seen a whale having tea with a horse?
I know it's very rare, of course.
Have you ever played the guitar with a cod?
Then you my friend, are totally and utterly odd!

Some people say I'm mad but it's all to do with my explanation,
All to do with my imagination.

Nia Roberts (11)
Our Lady & St Oswald's Catholic Primary School

As I Get Older

I grew as a baby
Learning much more along the way
From pram to buggy,
Learning each day.

The big day arrived,
I started my school
With lots of new friends
And teachers to greet.

Junior classes,
I was very worried,
But soon decided not to be troubled.

Leaving school,
Missing teachers and friends,
Will be a journey right to the end.

Sophie Jennings (9)
Our Lady & St Oswald's Catholic Primary School

My Mum

My mum's smart, kind and witty
I also think she's really pretty.
She likes to care for us and Dad
Although sometimes we're very bad.
She sorts the house and food and clothes,
How she has the time, nobody knows!
She goes to work, whilst we're at school,
But her uniform's not very cool.
In hospital, she's a physio
Treating injured people, you know.
She's a taxi when we want her to
Drive us here and there, so much to do.
But I like it best when it's time for bed
And we've brushed our teeth
And the prayers we've said.
And she comes to us and hugs us tight
And she gives us all a kiss goodnight.

Catherine Holbrook (9)
Our Lady & St Oswald's Catholic Primary School

Spiders

Spiders give girls the creeps
And give some boys a shiver
But one of the things spiders hate
Is being pushed down a river.

Some spiders are jumpy and big
And some of them are tall,
Some of them are sort of lumpy
and some of them are small.

Tobie Clarke (8)
Our Lady & St Oswald's Catholic Primary School

Winter Weather

Winter is cold and frosty,
Everything is covered in snow.
The day is long and cold, like a river of ice.
Nothing is colder than a winter's day.
The fingertips of people go as red as fire,
On a cold winter's day, the fire is glittering.
The frost on the grass is as shiny as diamonds.
Children playing in the snow having snowball fights.
Jumping in snow piles, like there's no right or wrong.

Jack Palmer (8)
St John's RC Primary School, Bridgnorth

Winter

In the cold winter night, snowflakes fall,
Snow glistens in the moonlight.
I get up and run as the blizzard comes.
I glide across the ice.
Snowballs hit the windows, rapidly,
The blizzard gets worse as windows smash.
Ice sticks out as sharp as a knife.
Ice shines.

Gary Ball (8)
St John's RC Primary School, Bridgnorth

A Winter's Day

I like the cracking of the snow that is under my feet,
I like the firing of the snow that comes from the sky.
I like the puddles that have frozen over,
So that you can have great fun skidding on them.
I like the robins that fly around in the winter,
I like the trees that are covered in a white sheet of snow.

Michael Peter Daw (9)
St John's RC Primary School, Bridgnorth

Seasons

Winter brings the cold and snow,
Makes our feet and fingers glow.
In front of our windows, snowflakes cascade down
Then slowly, on the front lawn, they begin to drown.
The snow and ice brings excitement,
The children are frisky and enlightened.
The snow glistens on the front lawn,
It stays there from noon, right until dawn.

Winter slips slowly into spring,
We love all the new things that it brings
Little lambs are seen whilst they leap,
The beautiful little offspring of the sheep.
The new season brings new creations,
As the animals come out of hibernation.
The daffodils bloom and come to life,
The other flowers join in their strife.

Spring turns into summer,
And we play happily with one and other.
The children love to eat cool, ice creams,
Under the sun's scorching beam.
Summer's the time for happiness and joy
For every girl and boy.
The holiday is a time for fun
And playing underneath the sun.

As it turns to autumn it starts to get colder
And the hunters by the minute are starting to get bolder.
The deciduous leaves begin to fall
But the evergreen trees stay standing strong and tall.
It's windy and wet all day long
And the hummingbird no longer sings his soothing song.
The farmers are harvesting their long, growing crop
And once they've started, they never do stop.

Emma McLoughlin
St John's RC Primary School, Bridgnorth

Winter Season

Snow as cold as ice,
Floating like a feather.
Ice as sharp as knives
Cutting into hearts.
Frost spreading round the world
Like a sea of ice.
Icy roads making cars skid
Snowballs hitting walls and windows.
Windows frosting over,
Grass and cobwebs sparkling in the sunlight.
Coldness cutting into skins,
Leaves and trees frosting over,
Spitting snowflakes, falling down.

Alice Victoria Buszard (8)
St John's RC Primary School, Bridgnorth

A Weather Disaster

A hot summer's day melted my rubber ball
I fell asleep.
Then thunder came raining down on the grass,
Soaking the washing I'd just hung up.
I flew through the rain, grabbed my washing
And ran like the wind to my room.
I got changed and flopped on the settee and watched TV.
I got tired and went to bed,
Once a night I get a dream,
I find a hill, I start to climb
I get to the top,
Find a ruined castle which begins to crumble.
Then thunder claps
I look on my map but the castle is not there!

Stephen Murray (8)
St John's RC Primary School, Bridgnorth

Seasons

In spring, little lambs leap
They are the offspring of the sheep.
The spring brings new creations,
As the animals wake from hibernation.

In summer, we eat cool ice cream
Under the sun's scorching beam.
We can paddle in the pool,
We do that to keep us cool.

In autumn the air gets colder,
The hunters start to get bolder.,
We jump and play in the cool autumn air,
Our mums get cross because it messes our hair.

In winter, you can make frosty snowmen,
You can even make an ice den!
The air starts to get a cold breeze
And our fingers begin to freeze.
The ground is white with a sheet of snow,
The footprints like patchwork that Mummy has sewn.

Emily Harris (9)
St John's RC Primary School, Bridgnorth

Crispy Crunchy Snow

Frost in the Far East
Ivy crawling along the jewel encrusted snow,
The lake is frozen - if you fall in
You will be a frozen ice block.
The snow beneath, crispy and crunchy.
The winter air makes you wrap up warm,
The birds are calling whilst snow is falling
The ice is as hard as metal.

Conor Runswick (9)
St John's RC Primary School, Bridgnorth

Seasons And Weather

Every winter I come out
Every cold time I come out - I'm snow!
I fall from trees
With the windy breeze
I fall off rooftops when something is thrown at me.
The wailing trees blow me away
And move me somewhere else.

Maybe sometimes my friends come round
I call the frozen crackling phone,
Telling them where I've moved.
My friends Mr and Mrs Icicle say,
'Can I stay with you, the child's fridge
has broken down.'

Winter, winter, my favourite months
Snowball fights but just *not me!*

Olivia Parr (8)
St John's RC Primary School, Bridgnorth

Winter

Dreamy snowflakes float carefully down onto the frosted
window ledge and entwine the twisted willow.
The hearth crackles in the home and spreads warmth
around the house.
The twigs that lie on the footprinted ground are wrapped
in a fleecy blanket of snow.
Fathers scatter in the forest, collecting firewood.
Harassed mothers run to the shopping store to stock up on food.
Jackets are zipped and scarves wrapped,
as people scurry in the snow outside.

Alice Williams (8)
St John's RC Primary School, Bridgnorth

Seasons And Weather

S unny days in the boiling summer,
E aster showers bounce off the ground with a loud sound.
A nd in the winter, snow rains down on the mountains.
S now comes down like a big white blanket.
O n the grass, early morning dew sprinkles on the garden,
N asty weather comes in December
S howers in early September on the hills up high,

A lso lightning on bad days.
N ever sunny in cold November.
D elighted children making snowballs,

W indy days in the middle of spring.
E nter caves with icicles on the hanging roof.
A utumn days when the days get longer,
T o January where blizzards come and schools shut down.
H abitation where animals sleep.
E vergreen trees stay all round.
R ain in July, people all soggy.

James Burch (8)
St John's RC Primary School, Bridgnorth

The Snowy Day

Diamond ice, crackling snow
Cold like ice but smooth like snow
The winter's here,
Freezing noses as red as blood
Sparkling grass,
Snow covered houses.
Bin liners too cold for dustbin men to touch
Cats hiding under defrosted cars.

Neil Simmons (9)
St John's RC Primary School, Bridgnorth

Autumn Days

Autumn days are short and cold and are cloudy at night
Autumn days bring leaves shooting down and sycamore leaves
                                            twirling slowly down,
Autumn days are red and yellow that swirl about in the wind,
Autumn days have animals that collect their food and store it.
Autumn days are short and hard-working times.
Autumn days have bugs that recycle the leaves.
That is what happens on every autumn day.

Winter days

Winter days are short and freezing and it snows like Hell!
Winter days bring animals snoozing and trees are as bare as bark.
Winter days are as cold as ice.
Winter days bring snow flowing through the strong wind.
Winter days bring white and black that swirl in the strong wind.
That is what happens on winter days.

Thomas George Weston (9)
St John's RC Primary School, Bridgnorth

Seasons Poems

Snow as white as cotton
Ice cubes as sharp as knives
In the house it is nice and warm
When you go outside in
The snow, you see footprints in the snow.
It is freezing cold.
We could see the icy footprints,
Then everyone was making snowballs
We all had a snowball fight.
The wind was so strong
It became a blizzard.

Luke Thomas Owen (9)
St John's RC Primary School, Bridgnorth

Young Writers - Once Upon A Rhyme Shropshire

Sunlight And Moonlight

Sunlight, sunlight, sunlight bright,
Bright is light, light is bright.
The sun is bright and the moon is light,
Bright is light, light is tight,
People fighting, here comes lightning,
White is bright, so is the moon.

Winter, winter, winter's cold,
The pond is all iced and looks like glass,
Plus the children are all getting colds.
Not much sign of grass!
People wearing coats.
And lots of frozen moats.
Icicles dripping from the house.
No sign of a mouse.

Chloe Sherwood (9)
St John's RC Primary School, Bridgnorth

Walking In A Winter Wonderland

As I walk out of my home, flakes from the sky catch my eye,
I look so scared as the blizzard comes my way.
I look in the sky, a snowflake lies
And then a sweep of wind pushed off the roof.
'Oh no!' I cry. The snowflake fell on the spiky grass
As sharp as glass.
There it lies,
The snow, soft like fluffy dough
But as cold as ice cubes.
As I walk up the road, snowflakes fall from the sky
A sharp gate caught my eye
With ice-like blades of knives.

Rachael Carter (8)
St John's RC Primary School, Bridgnorth

A Winter Poem

Winter, winter, winter's cold,
The pond is as icy as glass,
Plus lots of children are getting colds,
Not much sign of grass!
People wearing coats
And lots of frozen moats.
Icicles dripping from the house,
No sign of a mouse!

Sunlight

Sunlight, sunlight, sunlight bright
Bright is light.
White is bright so is the moon,
People frightened, here comes lightning.
The moon is bright and light!

Ruth Brims (8) & Sarah Kilmister (9)
St John's RC Primary School, Bridgnorth

Winter Weather

Winter weather is cold and frosty
Everything is cold as ice,
The ground is covered with white frost
And snow.

The snowflakes fall on my warm hands
It makes them very cold,
I shiver when I feel the cold
It's as cold as ice,
The cold will go when I get home
To a warm fireside.

Kieran Swales (8)
St John's RC Primary School, Bridgnorth

A Hot Summer's Day

The sun is up, the sky is high
Birds come out to fly,
Trees growing in the sunbathing sky
Grass is growing bright green.
When you have seen apples growing on the trees
Bumblebees humming in the trees.
Flowers are growing like you've never seen before
Butterflies fluttering up high
Beautiful colours up high.
Blue sky
Green grass
Brown, brown bark from the trees.

Lucas Murray Johnson (9)
St John's RC Primary School, Bridgnorth

The Old Blue Barn

The wind blows in the cracks
of the old blue barn.
The sun's blaze is warm and
comforting in the summer.
The cold oak, bare with old wood
in the autumn's cold breeze.
The spring brings the blossom
on all the trees.
The children in the houses,
watch the pink wind flow like a river.

Pippa Stirling (8)
St John's RC Primary School, Bridgnorth

Betty

When Betty eats spaghetti
  She slurps
  She slurps
  She slurps.

When Betty is finished slurping
  She burps
  She burps
  She burps.

When Betty plays
  She breaks
  She breaks
  She breaks.

When Betty is finished breaking
  She pull,
  She pulls
  She pulls.

When Betty goes out
  She screams
  She screams
  She screams.

When Betty is finished screaming
  She cries
  She cries
  She cries.

Natasha Burnell (9)
St John's RC Primary School, Bridgnorth

Winter Weather

W inter is my favourite time of year,
  I cy weather pricks the air.
N aughty kids throw snowballs everywhere
T awny owls resting their heads
E legant swans fly overhead
R ushing water into ice

W eather is bitter, hiding the litter
E ggs in Hallowe'en are over
A nd what do you see in the crispy air?
T antrums get nowhere in the air.
H eaven's mother plucks the geese
E vermore and ever more
R oaring winds are going down.

Eleanor Frances Phillip (9)
St John's RC Primary School, Bridgnorth

Snowy Owl

Gliding through sunset
His bright eyes spot his big prey
His beak shuts tightly.

Jaydene Bell & Nathan Bentham (8)
St Mary's CE Primary School, Shawbury

Snowy Owl

Snowy is coming
Gliding through the winter air
Coat as white as snow.

Alice Clarke (7)
St Mary's CE Primary School, Shawbury

The Red Tailed Hawk

The beautiful tail
speeding through the deep blue sky
alone in the sun.

Jenny Partyka (7) & Jordan Anderson (8)
St Mary's CE Primary School, Shawbury

Snowy Owl

Snowy, so silent
Winter sky gleams in darkness
Looking for her prey.

Rosie Knight (9)
St Mary's CE Primary School, Shawbury

The Moon

At night it comes out
The moon is like ice crystals
At night it sparkles.

Hanna Gamble (8) & Cameron Beattie (9)
St Mary's CE Primary School, Shawbury

Tornado

He whizzes around
Rampaging across the land
Like a savage beast.

Megan Gamble (8) & Joshua Peck (9)
St Mary's CE Primary School, Shawbury

Falcon

It circles its prey
The killing machine pinpoints
The helpless target.

Callum Hillman (9)
St Mary's CE Primary School, Shawbury

Turkey Vulture

The black winged creeper
Hovers through the midnight air
In search of some food.

Andrew Rigby (9)
St Mary's CE Primary School, Shawbury

Snowy Owl

In the moonlit sky
Softly gliding through thin air
Hunting for his *prey!*

Christian Flood (8)
St Mary's CE Primary School, Shawbury

Snowy Owl

In the moonlit sky
Softly gliding through thin air
Hunting for his prey.

Shannon Holroyd (8)
St Mary's CE Primary School, Shawbury

Plants

Tender red rosebuds
Open in the bright sunshine
Shoot up from the ground.

George Taylor (9)
St Mary's CE Primary School, Shawbury

Snowy Owl

Flying in the snow
A white figure approaches
Then melts to thin air.

Jamie Turner (8)
St Mary's CE Primary School, Shawbury

Robin

In the crisp white snow
A red jumper for his breast
The winter cold bites.

Amy Shadbolt (9)
St Mary's CE Primary School, Shawbury

Barn Owl

Faster than the wind
Here comes a ghostly figure
Dining on its prey.

Hayley Berridge (7)
St Mary's CE Primary School, Shawbury

Eagle Owl

Beaks as sharp as knives
That is a powerful bird
He is amazing.

Marc Bolland & Abigail Lavis (7)
St Mary's CE Primary School, Shawbury

The Falcon

Faster than the wind,
Zooming through the air he goes.
But with victory.

Harry Daniels (9)
St Mary's CE Primary School, Shawbury

The Eagle

The deadly creature
Swooping down on his small prey
He strikes with no fear.

Amy Louise Cooper (8)
St Mary's CE Primary School, Shawbury

The Turkey Vulture

The black winged creeper
hovers through the midnight air
in search of the dead.

Lewis James Clarke (9)
St Mary's CE Primary School, Shawbury

The Eagle

Fast as a bullet,
Diving like a thunderbolt.
Pouncing on its prey.

Andrew Newman (8)
St Mary's CE Primary School, Shawbury

Eagle Owl

Hunting for its food
Looking for a helpless meal.
It has got its prey.

Ben Meade (9)
St Mary's CE Primary School, Shawbury

The Barn Owl

Flying by the barn,
Hovering in the dark sky,
Trying to catch mice.

Madeleine Robinson (8)
St Mary's CE Primary School, Shawbury

Eagle

Flying in the sky
Hunting for helpless prey
Fearlessly he kills.

David Bowden (9)
St Mary's CE Primary School, Shawbury

Snowy Owl

Slowly the snow falls,
Quickly he dives for his prey.
Ready for the kill.

Jasmine Oakley (9)
St Mary's CE Primary School, Shawbury

Snowy Owl

Gliding through the wind,
A white figure hesitates,
Suddenly - it strikes!

Molly Philpott (9)
St Mary's CE Primary School, Shawbury

Eagle

Circling its prey
Quietly he swoops down
As the darkness falls.

Daniel Tait (7)
St Mary's CE Primary School, Shawbury

Eagle Owl

At high speed he flies,
Down into the dark forest.
He swoops to his prey!

Georgina Hessey (9)
St Mary's CE Primary School, Shawbury

Barn Owl

A brown figure stares
He spots his poor helpless prey,
Dives in for the *kill!*

Bethany Foster (9)
St Mary's CE Primary School, Shawbury

Snowy Owl

Across the wastelands,
A ghostly shape in the gloom.
Silently he strikes.

Sam Kieran Day (8)
St Mary's CE Primary School, Shawbury

The Owl

Waiting in the barn
Red eyes glowing in the dark
Trying to catch mice.

Kimberley Rose Gillett (7)
St Mary's CE Primary School, Shawbury

Snowy Owl

White snow falling down
Feathers gleaming with silver
Hidden by the storm.

Chloe Warde (7)
St Mary's CE Primary School, Shawbury

The Sun And The Stars

The sun is so light
The stars give off a light
Both are very bright.

Caroline Knight & Will Thompson (9)
St Mary's CE Primary School, Shawbury

All The Seasons Of The Year

Spring is the time of growth,
For plant, trees and grass.
The cold winter's nights
Drift far, far away.

Summer is the sunny time,
I like it with a breeze.
It's nice on a beach in summer,
With the water and the sand.

Autumn is the fall
Of all the leaves on trees,
So they look bare,
It's turning colder now.

Winter is the time of hibernation
For all the sleepy animals.
Off to sleep they go,
And hear the cold winds blow.

And they are the four seasons of the year,
All summed up in one poem,
Spring, summer, autumn and winter,
There's a good thing about all.

Megan Bright (7)
Sir Alexander Fleming Primary School

Imagine A . . .

Imagine a boy
As small as a toy,
Imagine a float
As small as an oat.
Imagine a stake
As thin as a rake.
Imagine a wig
As fat as a pig,
Imagine a king
As noisy as a ping.
Imagine a pea
Covered in tea.

Tara Ellis-Jeffries (10)
Sir Alexander Fleming Primary School

The Full Moon

The full moon looks like
The letter 'O' floating in the air,
The sun shining, bright with no rays.
A golf ball ready to be hit,
A marble being tipped out of a bag.
Pepperoni ready to be put on a pizza,
A pupil staring at the stars.
Buttons just being sewn onto a cardigan,
A football just having been scored in the goal,
A fullstop just being written at the end of a sentence.
A red nose, shining like Rudolph's.

Sharna Cottey (8)
Sir Alexander Fleming Primary School

A View From My Window At Night

That night I looked out of my window,
I saw the dark night sky;
With crystal stars,
And the burning street lights.

Then I heard the roaring wind,
Blowing the clouds across the moon;
The twinkling moon,
Brightly shining moon up in the coal coloured sky.

Then I saw the light,
The break of dawn;
When all the owls go to sleep,
And the hedgehogs go safely to their homes.

Alex Hitch (10)
Sir Alexander Fleming Primary School

Fireworks

F is for fun, fun, fun, fun,
I   is for interesting fireworks in the sky,
R is for rockets, sparkling in the sky
E is for ear-aching loud in the sky.
W is for watching the stars in the sky,
O is for on the ground, lovely bonfire.
R is for people running to see lots of fireworks
K is for killing bonfire
S is for sinking wood in the bonfire.

Tilly May Perry (9)
Sir Alexander Fleming Primary School

A Poem About Animals In The Garden

The animals in the garden,
So lively and quick.
Some get to places in a tick,
There are a lot of animals you will see.

The snails and slugs like bushes and hedges,
Frogs like ponds and grass.
Hedgehogs are prickly to warn off other animals
They keep the circle of life.

The animals are *magnificent* creatures,
The spiders keep the flies away.
The worms mix the mud.
The animals are *magnificent* creatures
So love them and they will love you back.

Kelly Abbott (10)
Sir Alexander Fleming Primary School

My Day In The Jungle

I saw in the jungle . . .

A gorilla going bananas
And a big pack of koalas.
A big baboon,
Swinging on the moon.
A snake with eyes that gleam,
But if you see a crocodile
Don't forget to scream,
'Argh!'

Liam Melhuish (8)
Sir Alexander Fleming Primary School

A View From My Window At Night

The frosted moon glides gently in the never-ending sky
As the crystal-like ice smothers the grass,
Fog draws near, shrouding the treetops.
What's that? The screech of an owl
The squeak of a mouse soon leaves our house.

As I look forward with my eyes
I hear a hiss and a hoot echoing through the empty
Night sky.
As a train rolls by, a moth bitten rag comes twirling off the track,
And it gives me a last bellow from the whistle,
Onwards it travels though the mist into the night.

Kane Regan (10)
Sir Alexander Fleming Primary School

Environment

E nvironment
N ature
V egetation
I ncredible
R espect
O zone
N utritious fruit
M oorhen on the pond
E nergy
N atural
T rees.

Sean Davies (11)
Sir Alexander Fleming Primary School

A View From My Bedroom Window At Night

The view from my room at night,
it is as silent as my school at night,
apart from the engine rumbling,
or some boys on a scrambler bike,
and the tum-tum-tumbling
of a car screeching
down the lane.

All is silent
down the lane
until teenage boys in gangs
come out
and the acid smell
of smelly, strange cigarettes
fill the night sky.

An hour later,
darker still,
there is a clatter of shoes.
As the shoes' sounds
get further away,
the stench of cigarettes
leaves the silent lane.

Ben Perry (11)
Sir Alexander Fleming Primary School

A View From My Bedroom Window

As the cold wind whistles,
The trees swing to and fro,
The creaks in the darkness of a gate,
A star glows in the distance behind the misty sky,
The moon lights up the clouds,
The street is lit up by the street lamps but no one passes,
The conifer trees' shadows next door are dancing in the wind.

Shaun Coldicutt (11)
Sir Alexander Fleming Primary School

A View From My Window At 9pm

As I look out into the dark,
The dark looks in at me,
All the cars that are parked,
Motionless and still.

If I look right down
I see my garden
With plants that my mum grows
And grass and a dark blue shed.

If I look to my left,
I see the school field
And the school
With lots of windows.

If I open my window,
I hear the whistling,
Whistling of the wind,
And a breeze rushes in.

The breeze is cold,
And it cools me down,
So I get colder and colder,
I shiver.

I close the window,
And warmth rushes through me.
As the wind rushes around outside,
I slip into bed and off to sleep I go.

Jamie Bright (11)
Sir Alexander Fleming Primary School

Sand Cinquain

Sand is
Blowing away
By the howling strong wind
Getting washed away by the sea
Calmly.

Laura Churm (9)
Sir Alexander Fleming Primary School

A View From My Window At 8.30pm

As I glare out of my window at 8.30pm,
I realise in hours it will be am,
I see the whizzing cars,
and above them the stars
as they twinkle and glow
like the icy puddles below.
I see lights shine brightly
from the houses across
from where I am,
and on the rocks I see green moss.
The moon is silver,
it lights up my street like the cold, glittering sea.
The stars are like drawings on a black piece of paper.
The lamp posts are shining on the gardens of my street,
and I see Amy, the nice girl whom I met last week.
She doesn't say a word to me,
as she wants to be as quiet as can be.
But I feel tired, and it's nearly 9.15,
I close my eyes and I remember back,
the things that I've seen.

Casey Wells (10)
Sir Alexander Fleming Primary School

The Cloud

Once I sat upon a cloud,
I shouted out loud,
What has this world become?
Planet Earth I come from,
Earth is different now,
It needs a big, big help,
We need to save it.

Jessica-Paris Stokes (9)
Sir Alexander Fleming Primary School

A View From My Window At Night

As the night fades away,
It's getting lighter and lighter,
But while it's dark and lonely,
The stars twinkle like a crystal balm
And the lights are a burning fire.

In the grass I hear a noise; I think it is a grasshopper,
It croaks and croaks until it's asleep.
But then I see the light; the light comes in,
I hear the birds twitter about
As they come back from hunting
And then there is a silent night.

Bethany Luter (10)
Sir Alexander Fleming Primary School

When I Look Out Of My Bedroom Window At Night

I can't get to sleep at night-times, because buses go past,
When I look out of my window,
The moon shines down
And the foxes and the fox cubs are playing on the grass.

As the night-time goes by,
The morning is coming,
The birds are tweeting,
The people are awake.
The street lights are turning off,
The foxes will soon come out again.

Nicole Doyle (11)
Sir Alexander Fleming Primary School

A View From My Bedroom Window At 9.45pm

The starless sky is deep and blank,
Time is standing still.
The world is too dark to see, so dark and black,
Not a movement. It is too empty.
No lights but a slight glow from houses,
With people snuggling down.
The shadows become objects
In our Telford town.

The sky is moonless,
The world is asleep, dreaming of future days,
Everything's silent, the sky so deep,
It's empty and lonely and calm.
Time is stopped 'til morning time,
When the sun will shine brightly down.
The world will seem to come alive again,
Until the night is nigh.

The sun will set, the moon will rise,
If it is there at all.
The stars will twinkle, the clouds will play,
The night will be alive.
The day will come, the moon will fade
Right into the sky.
The world will be in day again,
'Till the sun will die.

Lisa Simpkins (11)
Sir Alexander Fleming Primary School

Different Habitats

In the rainforest every day - it's a struggle to survive.
Plants are growing big and strong,
With animals roaming inside.

In the woodland, the soil there is moist.
Mighty oaks and proud elms
Rule the woodland large.

In the ocean, the reef is beautiful,
Multicoloured fish swim around, some in shoals and some alone.
Sharks and barracudas are the predators of the sea.

In the meadow, the grass is tall,
And butterflies fly around.
Mini-beasts rule the ground, and birds the sky.

At the Pole, the temperature is cold,
And only warm enough for polar bears and Arctic foxes.
Igloos are icy and the snow is deep.

In the desert there is nothing there,
Apart from stretches of sand.
The only animals are camels and gerbils.

There you have some of the habitats of the world,
Some are being destroyed and we have to help,
Everything little is something big.

Andrew Stewart (11)
Sir Alexander Fleming Primary School

A View From My Window

'Twas windy and cold at 2am,
The bush rustled in the wind.
Was it a cat or a rat
Or was it the wind?
My next-door neighbour's gate blown over,
Bang it went
When it hit the wet pavement.
I looked up and stars were shining
Like a golden crystal ball.
They shone in the sky.

The bins had blown over, *clash! Clang!*
The cats from the street above went scavenging
In the bins for scraps of food.

Jordan Needle (11)
Sir Alexander Fleming Primary School

A View From My Window

The street light is like a sparkling star,
The grass is like a field,
The sky is like a dark grey cloud,
The stars are like glitter.

The wind is like a howling storm,
The breeze is like thunder,
The moon is like a big, round balloon,
The clouds cover the silvery moon.

The crisp packets rustle,
The garages shake with boys kicking footballs,
The gate opens for me,
Ready to wake.

Kimberley Roberts (10)
Sir Alexander Fleming Primary School

A View From My Bedroom Window

It was a dark, cold night
When I looked out of my window
At the silent streets below.
The streets were shining
And the stars were all smiling
As I watched from my bedroom.

The moon was twinkling as bright as could be,
As all the people were fast asleep.
The wind was blowing through the grass
And then I saw the frost on the ground.
The aeroplane's lights were shooting brightly
As it flew across the dark sky.
The beaming stars were high above
Then the big, bright moon came into sight.

Layla Hughes (11)
Sir Alexander Fleming Primary School

A View From My Window At Night

There I stand looking through my window,
Like someone is looking into a dark, dim hole
Wondering what is there.
Every so often you see someone walking down the street
And you think about what it's like at the bottom of the night.

You see the stars at the top of the sky
And wonder what's behind them.
I always think there's nothing,
But who knows at night.

As the wind blows in the trees,
It makes you feel the day is over.
It's sad in a way
To say goodbye to the day.

Daniel Gill (11)
Sir Alexander Fleming Primary School

The Moon Watch At 8.30

As I looked out of my window at 8.30,
I could see that the moon had come out quite early,
It was dark and chilly
And the moon was shining brightly.
The stars were just coming into sight,
I looked down at the silent streets below me and
There was a group of people
Walking under the shining moon
And the glittering stars.

Just show me
The shining moon and the glittering stars again so
I looked up and it was still there shining down below me.
The people passing by in the silent night.
I could hear their muffled voices
As they walked past my shining gate
That reflected off the moon.

Jaimelea Morgan (10)
Sir Alexander Fleming Primary School

The Black Cat

I have a black cat
Who tries to catch the bat
Which flies around my garden
Catching all the gnats.

She caught it once
And brought it to the house,
She dropped it quick because my mom would shout,
My mom picked it up and put it outside,
If flew so quickly she couldn't see its eyes.

Katie Jane Webb (8)
Sir Alexander Fleming Primary School

A View From My Window At Night

A street light is like a burning fire,
The grass is like a swampy field,
A dark grey sky,
The stars are like candles.

The wind is howling fearlessy over the treetops,
A cat walks over my garden,
A car goes by,
Then, about 10 minutes later, another.

The gate rattles,
A football hits the garage, *crash!*
The boys make a loud noise,
The boys scrape their feet on the ground.

The clouds cover the silver moon,
The breeze is like thunder,
The crisp packets blow slowly by,
A sweet wrapper scuttles past too.

Sarah Westwood (11)
Sir Alexander Fleming Primary School

My Cat

My cat is a very cheeky cat
a very cheeky little brat.
I know she's still a little child
but her behaviour is rather wild.
She jumps from the shed to the garage to the trees,
and chases after the birds and the bees,
She steals my dad's chair and bites my mom's slippers,
she quite likes her cat food but prefers salmon and kippers.
But she's so soft and furry and loving and kind,
and I love her so much so I really don't mind.

Emma Baker (8)
Sir Alexander Fleming Primary School

The Football Match

First half

The match is boring,
The fans still roaring,
Wolves score,
And the players want more,
The crowd goes wild,
And act like a child.
That wasn't very mild.

Second half

The crowd is roaring,
But the match is getting boring,
Again Wolves score,
But now Man U don't want anymore,
The people are excited,
And the players are delighted,
It seems like the crowd has just ignited.

After match

The crowd are celebrating,
But they don't hurry up to accelerating,
Some of the crowd slip and slither and get all slimy,
The rest of the crowd say, 'Blimey.'
As a snake bites 'em.
The people who didn't say, 'Blimey,' go all numb,
So they start drinking rum.

Balvinder Singhru (10)
Sir Alexander Fleming Primary School

A View From My Bedroom Window At 10.30

As the cold wind roars,
The trees sway to and fro
And the leaves blow off and around.
Cuckoo! Cuckoo! Cuckoo! Cuckoo!
Goes the cuckoo clock next door.
Within a minute it's stopped and
All is silent
Except the wind whistling and roaring.

The moon is bright and brilliant,
She's beautiful, full of life
And sparkling stars are scattered all over the sky.
The misty clouds pass across her,
To make her dull and gloomy.
But she will come through again
As she is too bright to be shut away.
She brightens the night for occasional passers-by,
But they do not appreciate her
As they are wrapped up in their own secret thoughts.

As I look through my bedroom window,
I start to feel quite sleepy.
I feel I can't stay awake anymore,
So I crawl into my bed,
I lie awake and think about the things
I've heard and seen this night
And eventually I fall asleep and dream.

Michelle Ellis (11)
Sir Alexander Fleming Primary School

The Cricket Match

I went to a cricket match,
And saw one of the players
Make an amazing catch.
What a great sight to see,
Until I got stung by a bumblebee.

It stung really hard,
It would have been OK if it hadn't scarred.
Back to what happened in the game,
It ended in a great flame.

The game came to an end,
Then I met up with my friends,
We all had a great time
And decided to go to mine.

Sahir Hussain (9)
Sir Alexander Fleming Primary School

Sunshine

Without the sun in the sky how cold it would be,
With no cover at all, what would you see?
We would all have red noses from here to the sea,
With no light in the sky to turn night into day,
How would we know it was time for play?
With no sun in the sky, how dull life would be,
The sun keeps us warm, it turns night into day.
It tells us it's time to get up and play.
It warms the Earth, it helps plants to grow.
But best of all, it melts the cold snow.

Erica Ford (9)
Sir Alexander Fleming Primary School

Hungry Harry

Hungry Harry ate cousin Larry,
He ate my stew and my brother too!
He went to my class and ate a young lass,
When he came home, he ate some foam.
He went to the park and ate a lark,
He went on the roof and ate Mr Booth.
He went to the town and ate a clown,
He went to the shops and ate their lollipops.
He started to fall so he ate a wall,
He felt sick so he ate a tick.
Hungry Harry grew very ill, he had to eat a terrible pill.
He ate no more for a very long time,
To hungry Harry it felt like a crime.

Robert Carter (9)
Sir Alexander Fleming Primary School

Alton Towers

A is for adventure all day long,
L is for log flume, you will splash,
T is for tea cups where you spin round and round,
O is for Oblivion, you almost hit the ground,
N is for Nemesis, you will turn upside down.

T is for towers tumbling down,
O is for over and over again,
W is for wild and wonderful day,
E is for enjoyment all the way,
R is for Ripsaw where you twist and turn,
S is for skyward to make your tum churn.

Sophie Louise Parker (9)
Sir Alexander Fleming Primary School

Winter Poem

W inter is very cold,
 I n the frost I shake,
N earby is a bit of a snowflake,
T he day sure is short,
E venings are dark,
R ivers are almost made of ice.

Sam Blaney (8)
Sir Alexander Fleming Primary School

The Moon

Moon beams softly through the night
sends golden rays of light
that glimmer and glisten like raindrops fresh and bright.
The moon's smiling face, like an old friend
that gazes gently down
and looks upon us in the town
each and every night.

Alex Bliss (8)
Sir Alexander Fleming Primary School

Dragons

D ragons are very
R are and very big
A nimals. They're all nearly
G one except for
O ne. At the end of a curse but
N ow dead.

Conner Protheroe-Jones (8)
Sir Alexander Fleming Primary School

My Rabbit

A rabbit is a friend that you can cuddle
And when you put it down, it runs into a puddle.
After you've chased it down the path
You have to put it in the bath.
You dry it very well,
Now it doesn't smell.
Put it in its cage and make sure it's shut
So it does not get out of its hut.

Michelle Bowker (8)
Sir Alexander Fleming Primary School

Football Crazy

A football is like
a clock zooming through the air.
A football is like
a sun round and hot.
A football is like
a moon glowing in the air.
A football is like
a golf ball, only bigger.

Anthony Booth (9)
Sir Alexander Fleming Primary School

Sunshine Cinquain

Sunshine
Shining brightly
Sunshine shining away
Sunlight moves softly and brightly
Peaceful.

Harpal Kaur (9)
Sir Alexander Fleming Primary School

Sleepless Night

Tossing and turning,
I'm as hot as Hell,
Suddenly I hear a noise,
I wake in terror,
I hear a squeal across the
Blackboard.
I hear a whistling noise,
Around my bed,
I hear footsteps
Clattering up the stairs,
I get out of bed,
Open the door,
Guess what I see?
It is my kitten
Holding up her paw.

Lauren Mason (9)
Sir Alexander Fleming Primary School

Can't Sleep

There is a creaking of the floorboards,
A bursting of the pipes!
I hear a gunshot!
I picture myself lying dead with a bullet in my head.
Another gunshot. I wonder why!
I slink over to the window,
A person with a pistol is approaching the door!
My mum and dad are imprisoned in a deep sleep!
A hero appears to save the day!
I mustn't get in his way -
Everything's OK now, it was just a dream.

Cameron Roberts (9)
Sir Alexander Fleming Primary School

The A To Z Of Cats

A is for a stupid cat
B is for bedtime cat
C is for come home cat
D is for don't open the cat flap
E is for every cat eats
F is for funky fighting cats
G is for giant cats
H is for hip hop cool cats
I is for ice-cold cats
J is for jazzman cats
K is for kat-knip
L is for long-lasting cats
M is for moving grooving cats
N is for naughty cats
O is for outrageously stupid cats
P is for pie-eating cats,
Q is for quiet cats
R is for rifle shooting cats
S is for Smudge - the best cat
T is for time wasting cats
U is for ultimate cats
V is for Venus cats
W is for wanna be a cat leader
X is for excellent cats
Y is for yucky cats
Z is for ze ultimate creature - cats.

Izaak Addis (10)
Sir Alexander Fleming Primary School

A View From Window At Night

When I looked out of my window
it looked kind of dark
the moon shone brightly
over the treetops
the dotted stars scattered all over the sky
I looked onwards and
the moon looked round and clear

The fire was burning downstairs
it was getting rather cold
I looked once again into the sky
and to my amazement a bright star left
a beam in my eye
the moon looked frosty
and as the clouds covered the moon
it got kind of dull and looked like a dark, gloomy sky
the bright star looked like a silver crystal

The grass had dark footprints
and on my door I saw a dark smudge clear as crystal
the moon looked like it had got bigger
it got colder so I shut my window ledge for another night.

Chris Watton (11)
Sir Alexander Fleming Primary School

My Horse

My horse is bright and brave.
A golden silky wave
We took a trip around the world.
Now his mane became all curled.
He gets jealous when I feed my bunny.
His colour is just like honey.

Hannah Lister (9)
Sir Alexander Fleming Primary School

Green

Green is a colour,
Silky and soft.
Green is a leaf,
On a new glowing tree.
Green is a blanket,
That is a front lawn.
Green is the lush
Growing grass.
Green is a colour that
Glints in the sun.
Green is a wonderful colour,
Tell everyone,
And last of all,
Green gets me out of my long winter's nap.

Bethany Nenshi (9)
Sir Alexander Fleming Primary School

The Safari

I went to the safari,
In my Ferrari,
I went past a lorry,
Saw a woman with a Tesco trolley,
Her name was Molly,
In the Tesco trolley she had a lolly,
I said, 'Can I have that lolly Molly?'
There was a monkey in a brolly,
Who stole all her lollies,
The lion saw a monkey riding on a donkey.

Mandeep Singh (9)
Sir Alexander Fleming Primary School

The Life Of Paglo

There was an old woman called Paglo,
And people said she was hag-lo.
She was very old,
She was going bald,
So people called her an old bag-lo.

One day Paglo found some old knives,
So she threw them at some beehives,
They went into the sea,
Then she had her tea,
And when they came out they had wives.

Then the wives, they wanted a divorce,
Because the husbands all wanted a horse,
But they didn't sign the paper,
They said 'Maybe later,'
And it was a happy ending, of course.

Gurpreet Johl (10)
Sir Alexander Fleming Primary School

My Imaginary Pet

He's as ferocious as a lion,
He's as big as an elephant,
He's as playful as a dog,
He's hairy like a bear,
He can fly like an eagle,
He's got sharp claws like a hawk,
He's as fast as a cheetah,
He's got a shell like a turtle,
But best of all he loves you.

Ciaran Ransom (10)
Sir Alexander Fleming Primary School

Tanks

The tanks went to war
protected the flank.
They said they would win
using brute force.
Manoeuvre with force
a deadly rampage through the
enemy lines.
They got to Hitler!

Thomas Betts (8)
Sir Alexander Fleming Primary School

Spiders

Spiders are black!
Spiders are scary!
Spiders are very smelly!
Plus *hairy!*
They come out at midnight
To bite and to give you a fright!

Angela Kelly (9)
Sir Alexander Fleming Primary School

The Sun

The sun is like a big smiley face
The sun is like a big bouncy ball
The sun is like a big round circle
The sun is like a big round planet.

Zara Davis (9)
Sir Alexander Fleming Primary School

The Scary Frog

The frog smells of rats,
The frog is all lumpy,
The frog lives in the pond,
And its tongue is all bumpy,
The frog is all big,
The frog is disabled,
The frog has got red eyes,
The frog is noisy, blup, blup, blup,
As he jumps the sweat comes off,
Oh the scary frog.

Natasha Turner (8)
Sir Alexander Fleming Primary School

Waterfalls

W ashing waves,
A ngry,
T errific,
E xciting,
R emarkable,
F antastic,
A nd
L arge,
L ovely,
S teep.

Rebecca Harris (9)
Sir Alexander Fleming Primary School

Bored

Bored, bored,
I'm bored out of my head.
I'm bored by the window,
And bored on my bed.

I've read all my books,
I've played all my games.
I'm fed up of thinking of
fortunes and fames.

I don't want to eat,
I don't want to drink.
I don't want to sleep,
And I don't want to think.

I'm not really happy,
I'm not really sad.
If I don't do something,
I'm gonna go mad.

Eleanor Rogers (9)
The White House School

Summer Sun For Kids

The sun is shining yellow and bright,
Shining down, lots of light.
Kids splashing in the pool,
Jumping down into the cool.
People playing different things,
Children playing on the swings.
Slides, see-saws at the park,
Better go home, it's getting dark.
Get in bed and wrap up tight,
Mind the bedbugs don't bite.

Shahid Latham-Remtulla (10)
The White House School

The Doodlebug And The Car

Black, icy roads
Dismal clouds hide the sun
A car zooming along *bang!*
Oh no!

Into the fence
And hit against
A doodlebug
Who gave them a hug.

'Ahh, you thug,' I cried,
'You broke our car and gave it a hug,
We nearly died,
You should get fried,
In vinegar and batter.'

'I'm not your friend,'
Yelled that doodlebug fiend,
'You should be sent to prison.'
'Ahh!' the doodlebug cried
And he . . . burnt up fried.

Sam Hall (10)
The White House School

My Birthday

It's my birthday today,
Hooray! lots of presents for me.
A new bike and game,
But nothing the same.
All my friends will come,
And then we will have lots of fun.

Joshua Maddocks (10)
The White House School

My Day

I woke up this morning
and I heard my sister snoring.
I went to school
obeying the rules.
I sat at my table
and read out a fable.
I picked up my pencil case
and did up my shoelace.
I started my work
and we had some maths homework.
I went home
and got out my comb.
I brushed my hair
and cuddled my teddy bear.
I'm going to be fed
then I'm off up to bed.

Aimee Hargreaves (9)
The White House School

Snow

Snow comes down like
White sheets falling in the air.

Wrapping up in warm
Coats, gloves and hats too.

Children sledging everywhere
Throwing snowballs at one another.

Running in the snow
Crunch, crunch below.

Eventually having to go home
Oh no!

Laura Sears (10)
The White House School

My Mate And His Mammals

My mate has got a mixture
A whole bunch of mammals.
He's got a pig
Who did a little jig
He wears a purple wig
He wears rags
And lives in a bag.
He even gnaws on a hag!
But he's got a mouse
Who went on strike
From riding a motorbike
He sits in a mini house
Eating a mini louse!
He also has a bunny
Who was incredibly funny
He's got a big tummy
And sucks on a dummy.

William Jackson (9)
The White House School

Stars

We see tonight stars, stars.
Yellow stars,
Shooting stars,
But my favourite stars tonight
Are red and blue.
Oh no! That can't be right,
Uh-oh! It's a spaceship.
There is a star in the hall,
A star in the bath,
So watch out, it might come
Creeping up your path.

Georgina Page (10)
The White House School

Seasons

W hat a great time we will have,
 I t is snow time again.
N ow wrap up warm,
T ime to sledge.
E venings are very dark,
R inging Christmas bells.

S inging baby birds,
P lant your flowers today.
R inging bluebells,
 I t is a beautiful sight.
N ow new plants are growing,
G etting lighter days.

S un cream is needed,
U mbrellas away, hooray!
M ay get burnt today.
M ore games to play,
E veryone having fun,
R ainy season has gone.

A ll the trees lose their coats,
U ncovering the bare tree branches.
T rees are cold,
U nderfoot, mountains of leaves.
M ornings will get darker,
N ot a green leaf in sight.

Emily London (9)
The White House School

The Blade Of Death

Here I am made of pewter and bone,
I sit here all alone,
My job is to kill; but it is not a thrill
To see the victim killed against their will.

The priest he uses me to kill
A victim on the stone so still,
He is the dragon of flames, but no one complains,
For he put death in his games.

The victim he sits like a worm,
The victim will slide and squirm,
He sits in demise, as he is watched by the eyes,
And sacrificed under the scarlet skies.

It is the difference between death and life,
The worm in agony and strife,
He has the power of the Celts, like a puppy he yelps,
But for the worm; no help.

Stephen Vincent (10)
The Wilfred Owen Primary School

Aztec Sacrifice

I burn up and am ready to strike the victim.
I rush across the chest like a hissing snake.
I screech like chalk on a blackboard.
The victim is like a rat
Twitching
And the cut of the knife is painful and sharp.
The priest is like the hiss of a dead snake.
And the venom runs through the servant.
I was the blade cutting the chest.
I was covered in blood.
The priest dug me in.
The victim fell like a whirlwind and
settled like an empty box.

Laura Farrall (10)
The Wilfred Owen Primary School

The Sacrifice

I am the sacrifice table.
People come with their gory death.
Blood-spattered, frail guts sprayed all over me.
I'm as old as an ancient shrivelled-up river
With long-lost skeletons in.
I'm all alone in the middle of the gold-plated temple.

Up huge steps.
I'm a jagged and cracked old sacrifice stone.
Victim after victim, knowing they're about to *die*.
The smell of blood from the victim, smoke of the fire.
The priest is a cheetah.
He sees his prey and roars.

The victims are little helpless kittens,
Trying to escape the painful death.
But the chains are too powerful,
The weak and poor victim is helpless.

Javan Gask (11)
The Wilfred Owen Primary School

The Deadly Knife

Crawling calmly the sly lizard snarls
slithering and slurping like a boiling pan.
I am lying lifeless on my stone platform
my stained blade dripping cold blood.
Before my eyes I glimpse the fearful victims
terror-stricken. The sufferers shake like moving earth.
Yelling vague voices echo in the air.
The whimpering, wailing cries are heard for miles around.
Foul-smelling ancient blood fills the still air.
The stinking rotten skin stays attached to the ground.
The quivering, quaking rodent shakes before me
jittering nervously like a stone tumbling down steps.

Jamie Roberts (10)
The Wilfred Owen Primary School

Aztec Poem

The eagle swept the body
slashing through the fabric
like claws. The object felt the
priest's cold-blooded hands.

The sparrow curled up into
a ball and he whimpered
into the coffin. The villainous
knife was a cruel bottle of venom.

The knife smelt the stench
of his sentenced victim. I
hear the cry of a crew
on a sunken ship.

The fresh knife slices, slashes
through the organs. The priest
digs through the bleeding body like
a dog hunting a bone.

Kristian Timmins (10)
The Wilfred Owen Primary School

Aztec Sacrifice

The gold glitters, blisters, like the sun
As old as the temple, shining, bright
Reflecting the black bat
Teeth sharp as a vampire
Flapping and gliding
Silent as night

The burning torches flicker, twist
Smoke, bitter and acrid, coils upwards
The priests pray, crawling in the dark
Like the hedgehog sneaking in the night.

Robert Laird (11)
The Wilfred Owen Primary School

Sacrifice

Speedy, painstaking, disgraceful,
The tiger speeds like a drag racer,
Darting up the cold-blooded temple,
Ready for victims to be killed.

The bloodstained, deadly knife slits open the
Prey, drawing the enemy away,
The silence of screeching and shock
Surrounds Tenochtitlan,
The innocent people stand in amazement.

Cream of warm, wet blood weeps drops from
The tearful eyes of the panic-stricken victims,
The blade with the fresh, poisonous blood drips
Into its sacred coffin,
The blood-curdling scream of the terrorised
stops!

Alexandra Kesterton (10)
The Wilfred Owen Primary School

Aztec Sacrifice

Slithering slurping slowly the serpent stirs creepily.
He squelches like wet feet in murky mud.
I gleam, I shine under the glimmery sun
Positioned proudly on my stone throne.
In front of me I spy terrified prey.
The intimidated poor puppets fear the end.
Haunted horrific howls shouted into the air.
Poor creatures stutter like chilling ice.
Reeking putrefied fear fills the beaming sky.
Pungent rotting blood like ageing drains.

Jack Rogers (10)
The Wilfred Owen Primary School

Sacrifice

Yelling, screaming like a small mouse
Caught by a large and fierce cat.
The sounds of the knife cutting through
The eerie body of the victim sounds like a piece of paper torn up.
The rhythm of the priests pulping
Heart, thumping like a rat caught by
A vulture is sucking and gnaws on the victim.
The victim's heart, still pumping while being
Tugged out,
Is pouring out with cold, deadly blood,
Like juice splashing from a beetroot jar.
The axe, as old as a temple,
Is placed down on the bloodstained cloth.

Emma Whatmough (10)
The Wilfred Owen Primary School

Aztec Poem

The razor-sharp beak strikes its prey.
A gush of blood rapidly leaks
From the innocent sacrifice,
The eagle circles waiting, spying.

The thumping heart beats as it is ripped out
And ditched down the priest's mouth,
The mouse screeches, scaring weak tribes
But too late, the mouse is demolished.

I plunge into poor sacrifices
Cutting down their weak, dead bodies.
The dead carcass gets disposed of
Down the statuesque temple, falling.

Jake Sumner (10)
The Wilfred Owen Primary School

The Heart Taker

The vulture glides over his enemy,
He free-falls down at his weak defeated victim,
Then attacks with a razor-sharp beak,
He picks at the victim with hooked talons,
And plucks out his heart.

All around are screams of shameful victims,
And the sound of terrorised, suffering puppets,
Drawing the bats to drink the ruby-red blood,
The splash of guts on the glowing red floor,
Drying in the heat.

I smell the dead putrid stench of bodies,
I sense the rotting carcasses on the dead pile,
The temple steps are dripping with red wine,
I feel the pulping heart as I am plunged
Into the body.

Chris Hayes (11)
The Wilfred Owen Primary School

Deadly Aztec Sacrifices

Slowly the priest picks up the knife
As the victim lies there curled in rage,
A flickering flame flows to the priest's face.

The knife staggers to the victim.
As the shining blade cuts through the body
The heart of fear awakes like a running whippet
And lies like torn up paper.

The body lies in a coffin, cold and dead,
As the priest turns and walks away.
The sacrifice goes to a better place.

Sophie Price (10)
The Wilfred Owen Primary School

The Lizard

Slowly he creeps slyly
Up to the top of the temple
Like a sneaky crawling creature
Hunting in the silent desert.

I am sunshine crimson.
I burn, I smoke, older than time.
I smell the dead freshly dripping blood
And hear the weeping victim
Screaming with fear.

I see the priest slit open their middle
As the victim's heart is pounding
Like a boxer.
The heart-ripper grabs the pounding heart
And launches the weak victim.

Chloe Murphy (10)
The Wilfred Owen Primary School

The Tiger

Sneakily, stalking stealthily,
The tiger strikes the deer,
Like a needle piercing silk,
As a train racing through a tunnel.

I stand, I stare,
I watch the innocent prey,
Sacrificed by the tiger,
As a butcher carving pork.

I smell fear even from the tiger,
As the drum of the heartbeat pounds,
The wind rushes past,
Bringing the reeking stench of steaming sweat.

Naomi Lloyd (11)
The Wilfred Owen Primary School

Aztecs

The priest is a wolf ready to strike
He strolls along, thinking he's the best
And he growls like a lethal volcano
About to erupt.

The victim is like a helpless puppy
He runs around like a headless knight
And he yelps when he's hurt.

I am the knife. My blade is made of gold
My handle is made of wood, with silver embedded.
I am brand new and as deadly as venom
And I'm as painful as a crocodile tooth.

My handle is brown like a snake camouflaged on a tree
And my silver is as shiny as a magpie's nest.
My blade is gold with a bloodstained tip
Like a shark that has just bitten into its prey.

The wolf held me high in the air
And he dropped me into the victim's chest.
I can see body parts
I can see the heart thumping like a boxer
I can also see running blood like a deluge.

The wolf pulled me out of the puppy's chest.
I looked down, he was dead.

Mitchell Vaughan (11)
The Wilfred Owen Primary School

The Bloody Aztecs

Strutting proudly, the lion circles his prey
Roaring and snarling like a rumbling
Thunderous day.

Standing to attention I shine in the sunlight.

My blade drips murderously like ice melting.

The foolish victims bow before me.
Quivering.

Jamie Hartshorne (10)
The Wilfred Owen Primary School